My Testimony – Knowing God and Making Him Known

Joel Hitchcock

ISBN: 9798792696525

Table of Contents

Dedication 3

Introduction 3

Dreams come true 4

I decide to become a preacher of the Gospel 5

I find Jesus 9

My first sermon 11

I hear the voice of God calling me to the ministry 13

Like a raging fire 14

First missions' outreach 16

A *mini-revival* at my high school 17

Bible college 18

The Sick begin to get healed 20

Chaplain 21

Abducted 23

Going international 27

Heidi 30

Marriage and honeymoon 34

Revival services USA 37

Vision for international crusades 43

Victory in big crusade setback 49

Largest crowds 52

Financial victory 55

Pastoring a church 59

Our children 61

God delivers me from a dark season 66
Books 69
Christ in You 71
Jehovah Incarnate 73
The future 78
Other 79
    Suggested prayer of salvation 80
    What to do now? 81
    About the author 82
    Photo Album 83
    Contact information 105

Dedication

I dedicate this book to everyone that God used on the journey of my life – too many to mention by name.

I especially acknowledge my parents – Tony & Elaine Hitchcock, as well as my parents-in-law – Ronald & Linda Souder.

Last but not least – my darling wife Heidi, our children Anthony, Rebekah, Timothy, and Trey, and generations to come.

Introduction

My life has been filled with a multitude of supernatural encounters.

I titled my testimony, "Knowing God and Making Him Known," because I feel that my life has revolved around this statement. In the Bible, the word, *know* means to know God intimately, and to love Him. I could have called my testimony, "Loving God and Making Him Loved." Jesus said,

"Hear, O Israel; The Lord our God is one Lord: And thou shalt love the Lord thy God with all thy heart, and with all thy soul, and with all thy mind, and with all thy strength: this *is* the first commandment. And the second *is* like, *namely* this, Thou shalt love thy neighbour as thyself (Mark 12:29-31.)

To know God is to love God with all our heart, soul, mind, and strength. To make Him known is to love our neighbor as ourselves. I trust that my testimony will inspire you to also know and love God, and also to make Him known.

Joel Hitchcock, December 2021, Georgetown, Delaware, USA

Dreams come true

I looked upon those massive crowds in multiple countries. Multitudes upon multitudes stood there – eager to hear the Word of God, and to be healed of their infirmities.

To minister to them was truly a dream come true.

There they stood – thousands upon thousands of souls, coming into the Kingdom of God, and being healed of their diseases.

In Uganda, a rebel soldier who had been responsible for many killings, heard me say, "Even if you have killed someone, Jesus can save you!" He gave his life to Jesus, and God saved him.

In India, a crippled woman was carried to our crusade. Suddenly she saw a supernatural light flashing towards her, and heard a voice saying, "You are now healed." She stood up and walked. Jesus healed her.

In South Africa, a man told us that someone with a baseball cap came into his room, and told him to come to our crusade, and there he would be healed. Who could this strange visitor have been? Could it have been an angel of the Lord?

In that same crusade, someone saw Jesus standing beside me as I prayed for the sick, one by one. She said that as I laid my hands upon people, Jesus was laying His hands upon them with me.

In another crusade, a woman was brought to the crusade in a wheelbarrow, padded with a cushion. She stood up out of that wheelbarrow, and she was healed. Hundreds attended that crusade, and a local pastor told us his church was packed out with people that received Jesus in that crusade.

In Pakistan, a lady was carried onto the platform, because she could not walk. In an instant, Jesus touched here, and she was healed. At first, she had something like a seizure, then she stood up, and walked.

All pandemonium broke out in that crusade. The big tent was filled with thousands of souls, and they pushed forward for prayer. I saw two women slap each other physically in their determination to get to the front to receive prayer. Of course, I don't condone the slapping, but I appreciated their determination, and their faith that God would heal them.

In Venezuela, a crippled man stood up out of his wheelchair. This was an amazing miracle.

In one outreach in a tribal area, very far from civilization as we know it, Jesus showed up and healed the people. It started with the healing of a young man's deaf ear. He could hear perfectly in that ear. From that point onward, it seemed like every person we prayed for in that meeting was healed.

I could cite numbers, but I have moved away from doing that, not wanting to neither overstate nor understate the numbers. God knows the real numbers of those who came to Christ, and continue to be swept into the Kingdom of God.

I can tell story after story, and I pray that my testimony will bless you and stir you to dare to believe God for the impossible. Let me tell you *my story,* my testimony…

I decide to become a preacher of the Gospel

My family had been from South Africa for many generations. On both of my parents' sides I have great-great-grandparents who fought on the Boer side during the Anglo-Boer War (1899-1902,) and great-grandparents that had been sent to concentration camps during that time. My one ancestor of 6 generations ago installed the historical Hoets-organ the *Groote Kerk* in Cape Town.

However, I was born in England, because my dad and mom worked and lived there for a couple of years. I don't remember England, except for a faint memory playing with a toy. My earliest memories have been in South Africa. I have three siblings – my sisters Jessica and Jolene, and my brother Johnny. They are all the greatest people, and I love them very much.

I have vivid memories of my grandfather with my grandmother praying passionately on his farm. And when I was 8 years old, living on a resort located in the outback of South Africa, my friend and I talked about what we would be when we grew up. For some reason, we decided that we would be firemen by day and thieves by night!

Very impressed with this idea, I went to my mother to tell her about it. However, I first made her promise not to tell anybody, especially not my father. She promised, and I told her, "In the day time we will be firemen, and at night we will be thieves."

My dear mother was so gracious. She then said to me, "Okay Joel, I will not tell anybody, and I won't tell daddy. But just remember, Jesus sees everything you do. You cannot hide anything from Him. He sees and knows everything."

This came to me as great shock. I had not considered God and His omniscience. He knew everything. Not only would He know it when I steal, but He already knew that I had just decided that I would become a fireman in the daytime, and a thief at night.

I went back to my friend. I said, "Willempie, we cannot be firemen and thieves. My mom says that Jesus always sees us!" We talked about this for a while, and came to a solution: We would become preachers instead! It felt like this was the only way to appease God at this point. Of course, I now know we are not saved by our works, but only by faith and by the grace of God.

As humorous as this story may seem to be, it had a two-fold powerful impact on my life, my thinking, and my future.

First, it instilled within me a holy fear of God. Secondly, God in His providence was already at work to make me a preacher of the Gospel.

Let me touch on these two things briefly.

Firstly, about fearing God, the Bible says, "For we must all appear before the judgment seat of Christ, that each one may receive the things *done* in the body, according to what he has done, whether good or bad" (2 Corinthians 5:10, NKJV.)

It also says, "Then I saw a great white throne and Him who sat on it, from whose face the earth and the heaven fled away. And there was found no place for them. And I saw the dead, small and great, standing before God, and books were opened. And another book was opened, which is *the Book* of Life. And the dead were judged according to their works, by the things which were written in the books. The sea gave up the dead who were in it, and Death and Hades delivered up the dead who were in them. And they were judged, each one according to his works. Then Death and Hades were cast into the lake of fire. This is the second death. And anyone not found written in the Book of Life was cast into the lake of fire" (Revelation 20:11-15, NKJV.)

I am ever aware that I will stand before the Lord one day. On that day I do not want to hear Him say, "I never knew you: depart from me, ye that work iniquity" (Matthew 7:23, KJV.)

Rather, I want to hear those sweet and beautiful words, "His lord said to him, 'Well *done,* good and faithful servant; you have been faithful over a few things, I will make you ruler over many things. Enter into the joy of your lord.'" (Matthew 25:23, NKJV.)

Secondly, God was already at work to make me a preacher of the Gospel. And God has been working in *your* life too! You might not recognize it as clearly, or maybe you do, but keep seeking God, and you will see how He makes all things work together for your good.

The Bible says, "For we are His workmanship, created in Christ Jesus for good works, which God prepared beforehand that we should walk in them" (Ephesians 2:10, NKJV.)

I recognize that those *good works* are morally good actions that result from the powerful work of spiritual rebirth that comes from Christ, but I would also say that those good works are *great feats* and *amazing accomplishments* that God determined beforehand that you will exercise.

The wonderful thing is that God had them *prepared beforehand.* Like Psalms says, "And in Your book they all were written, The days fashioned for me, When *as yet there were* none of them" (Psalm 139:16, NKJV.) And, "Before I formed you in the womb I knew you; Before you were born I sanctified you; I ordained you a prophet to the nations" (Jeremiah 1:5, NKJV.)

Not all of us are called to be preachers. God calls us to be different careers, to accomplish different things, but it is all to build His Kingdom, to advance His Kingdom all over the earth, to win and disciple souls for Jesus.

Always ask God – what is Your plan for my life. God will show you.

I find Jesus

I accepted Jesus as my Lord and Savior when I was 10 years old.

Perhaps I did have a conversion experience at the time when I decided not to be a thief but a preacher, but I didn't actually confess Jesus as my Lord and Savior. I do remember do that when my Sunday School teacher led me in that prayer.

However, my strongest recollection of receiving Jesus was in response to a Gospel literature *tract,* a small booklet, which I read at age 10. I remember picking it up at a restaurant that we dined at while we were on vacation as a family.

At the end of the booklet, a question was posed, which demanded my attention. "If you did today, are you sure that you will go to heaven, that you have eternal life?" (Not the exact words, but something to that effect."

It then offered a suggested prayer of salvation. I knelt down in my room. I read the first line, closed my eyes, and repeated those words. I then opened my eyes, read the next line, closed my eyes again, and repeated those words. I continued to do this until I completed the entire prayer.

Once I was done, I was satisfied that I was now saved. I did not weep and cry, nor did I have any emotional experience. With only *childlike faith* I accepted Jesus, and received salvation.

Jesus said, "Assuredly, I say to you, whoever does not receive the kingdom of God as a little child will by no means enter it" (Mark 10:15, NKJV.)

If you have not yet received Jesus, how about doing so now. Just repeat these words with faith and sincerity:

"Dear God. I am a sinner. I cannot save myself. I need a Savior, and your name is Jesus. Thank you, God, that you came to earth to reach me and to save me. Forgive me of all my sin and wash me clean with the precious blood of Jesus,

I believe with my heart and confess with my mouth that Jesus died and rose again. I further declare that Jesus is my Lord from this day forward forever. You are my only God.

I open my life to you. Lord Jesus, come live in my heart. Please give me the power of your Spirit that I may live righteously. Thank you for giving me eternal life, and that when I die I will meet Jesus and live in heaven with you forever.

In Jesus' name I pray, Amen..."

Congratulations! If you prayed this prayer, God has accepted you. Jesus said, "All that the Father gives Me will come to Me, and the one who comes to Me I will by no means cast out" (John 6:37, NKJV.)

Of course, your journey with God doesn't end here. It has just begun. I listed some things to do after you receive Jesus at the end of this book, but simply put, you must be baptized, tell others about Jesus, attend church, make Christian friends, read your Bible, seek to be baptized in the Holy Spirit, develop a prayer life, and of course refrain from sinful habits.

I would like to say something about the tract – the little Gospel booklet I had read, which led me to pray the prayer of salvation. Whoever put that booklet in the restaurant had no idea that a little boy would pick it up, receive Christ, and go on to become an evangelist.

One of my Bible College lecturers told us that he accepted Jesus while sitting on his bicycle while listening to a street preacher. That preacher had no idea that little boy would grow up to become a very influential theologian, and train young men in the ministry.

"And let us not grow weary while doing good, for in due season we shall reap if we do not lose heart" (Galatians 6:9, NKJV.)

My first sermon

I preached my first sermon when I was 12 years old. Let me tell you how this happened.

I had a very happy childhood. I am so thankful to God for this blessing. I had a good dad and mom, and was raised in a wonderful environment. I spent the bulk of my childhood in the *Waterberg* region of South Africa.

My dad began to work at a holiday resort in the area as its manager. The resort was blessed with a natural hot mineral spring. Although the area was located in South Africa's outback, and was very quiet, things changed during the *peak season*, when thousands of people vacationed at the resorts in our area.

My dad made sure vacationers have a wonderful experience. For example, On Mondays there would be a mountain hike in the morning, and bingo at night, On Tuesdays a swimming gala in the morning, and a *money-or-the-box* show in the evening. On Wednesdays, *Boeresports*, complete with tug-of-war, jumping bag races, egg throwing, etc. The whole week was filled with fun. On Saturday morning a Mr. Muscles, Mr. Big Belly, etc. was held, with the final Ms. Resort, the winner who would be announced that evening.

At about 5pm on that same Saturday, there was a *Massa Braai* (big barbeque for all,) and then everyone would gather in the hall to receive their diplomas for the morning competition, and the winner of Ms. Resort was announced. This was followed by a dance.

Nothing happened on Sundays, because in those days *the Lord's Day* was still revered by most people in South Africa. However, if there happened to be a minister on vacation, my dad would ask him if he would preach on that Sunday. We heard many preachers from different denominational backgrounds share God's Word with us.

During one of those weekends, my dad didn't know what on earth he would do for that upcoming Sunday morning, because there was no preacher on vacation. Suddenly he lit up. "Joel, *you* want to be a preacher when you grow up, don't you?! Why don't you preach for us this Sunday?"

My response was instantaneous. Of course not. I was just a boy, and I would be scared stiff. But my dad assured me that I could do it. He even worked out my sermon for me. I practiced it a couple of times, and preached it on Sunday morning.

About 100 people showed up for the service. I was so nervous! I do remember I wore a brown *Speedo* sweat suit, and light brown *Grasshoppers* shoes. I also remember my mouth was so dry.

I do not remember clearly what I preached on, but something tells me that it might have been about John 3:16, "For God so loved the world, that he gave his only begotten Son, that whosoever believeth in him should not perish, but have everlasting life!"

This would become my thing to do on the resort. During peak season I would preach to people, and during off season I would preach to trees.

I would go into the woods with my Bible and tape recorder, and preach in the woods, with no one listening but the trees and birds. I would listen to my recordings, to see what it sounded like, and how to improve. I still have one of those tapes. I uploaded it to YouTube. I still had a kid's voice. It's in Afrikaans at https://youtu.be/MuGm5T3OkFI

I do remember once I was preaching up a storm. I was pacing back and forth, shouting at the trees to repent from their stubborn sin (or something like that). When I turned around, I saw three or four people promptly turning around and getting out of there! I guess they were on a nature trail walk, and instead of peace, they encountered fire and brimstone.

I also acquired thousands of Gospel literature tracts, and put them in the resort rooms. I wonder how many people received Jesus through those tracts.

I hear the voice of God calling me to the ministry

Although I had by now decided to be a preacher when I grew up, and although I had preached my first message, I had not clearly heard the call of the Lord to the ministry. I did not even think that there would be such a clear call. But when I was 13, I clearly heard the Lord's voice for the first time, and I was called to the ministry. Let me tell you how that happened.

I do not know how I received a newsletter from this evangelist. His name was Nicky van der Westhuizen. I had never heard of him, but the newsletter was filled with reports of the miracles that God was doing in his ministry. Those reports, and the corresponding photos amazed me.

The blind could see, the deaf could hear, and the crippled could walk. The evangelist encouraged his readers to set apart a day of fasting, for the power of God. I was so touched that I did it very soon. I fasted for an entire day. I only drank water. Needless to say, for a 13-year old, this was the longest day of my life! But dinner would be there by the end of the day.

As the day came to an end, I felt that I wanted to pray one more time before I eat. I went into my room and prayed. I asked a question: "Lord, do you really want me to become a pastor?" In the quiet of my room I experienced something I had never experienced before. I heard the voice of God.

I heard clear, concise words in my mind, but it felt like it came from my chest, and it was filled with power. The voice said, "Yes, my son, I want you to become an evangelist."

From that point on there was no turning back. I knew for sure that God wanted me to be a minister of the Gospel, and I began to pursue God like never before.

Like a raging fire

Once I realized God's purpose for my life, it was like a raging fire. There was no stopping. When I look back on my teenage years, I acknowledge that my passion and actions could only have been because of God.

Firstly, I read my entire Bible through from cover to cover at age 13, listened to preaching tapes, and did whatever I could to prepare me for ministry.

I began to pray very fervently. I would go into the bush, and on the mountain that overshadowed the resort, and pray long, long hours. I prayed hard and loud, calling out to God. Sometimes I would pray in my room.

Other times I would get a key to one of the bungalows, and pray throughout the entire night. I mean, I prayed hard and loud, and very passionately. I would begin sometime at about I guess 9 p.m. and pray throughout the entire night. The hardest time for me was at about 4 or 5 a.m. when I became tired. I would then pray more passionately, and pace up and down the bungalow. Just writing about those times reminds me of the precious moments I had with the Lord.

On one of these nights, I read Mark 16:17-18: "And these signs will follow those who believe: In My name they will cast out demons; they will speak with new tongues; they will take up serpents; and if they drink anything deadly, it will by no means hurt them; they will lay hands on the sick, and they will recover."

I know this is quite childish, but I made a deal with God. At first, I felt challenged, because it said that these signs would follow them that *believe*. That's it. If I believed, these miracles would follow – cast out demons, speak with tongues, etc., and what really stood out for me, "...they will lay hands on the sick, and they will recover."

I said to the Lord, "Okay, God. I am going to leave my Bible in this room, and go to the other room for a while. You can remove that verse out of the Bible while I'm gone. But if I come back and see the verse is still in the Bible, I am going to believe it fully, and act on it." As I said, this seems quite childish, but then again, I was just a child.

I left the room, and needless to say, when I came back to my Bible, the verse was still in there. It would have been a bigger miracle if God had actually removed that verse from my Bible. Nevertheless, since it was still in there, I was going to fully believe that verse.

I did not see immediate results. Partly because I didn't lay hands onto too many people. I was timid and shy. And God was still working in me. But those miracles, and healings, and demonstrations of the power of God would come. I will share that with you soon.

One night after midnight I climbed the mountain that overshadowed the resort. I was so hungry for God, and prayed there for a long time. There was a certain tree, which I asked God to set it on fire like when He appeared to Moses in the burning bush. It never happened, but I fire kept raging in my heart – a burning passion for God.

First missions' outreach

There was a community of black African workers that lived not too far from our house. By this time, I was 16 years old. I had watched Evangelist Reinhard Bonnke's videos, and began to have a burden for this community.

I let them know that I would hold a meeting at 3 p.m. at our house. Our house's back porch would be our platform. I made little benches with planks on bricks, about the size of those in Bonnke's meetings. I secured a translator, even though I could have preached to them in Afrikaans.

But at 3 p.m. not a single soul showed up. I looked through the window, paced around, and walked outside a little. My grandfather Oupa Dys lived with us at the time, and he called me over, and prayed for me. I remember his words well. Among other things, he prayed, "Lord, don't let this young man be disappointed today…"

Well, about a half hour later, they arrived. I guess we had about 20 people there. This was my first experience with *African time*, i.e. not showing up at the advertised time.

I preached with all my heart. My mom took a picture, which I cherish to this day. From that time on the workers gave me a nickname. They called me "Moruti." It means *Preacher*.

A *mini-revival* at my high school

I talked to my pastor about evangelism, and he gave me a manual called "Evangelism Explosion," by Dr. D. James Kennedy. It gave you step by step methods on how to share your faith. Here is a brief outline of how it works:

To begin the conversation, you would ask someone, "Do you know that God has a wonderful plan for your life?" Then you would ask, "If you died today, do you know for sure that you will most definitely go to heaven?

If they answer, "No," you would explain the Gospel to them, that they can actually know for sure that they will go to heaven if they accept Jesus Christ.

If they answer "Yes," your next question would be, "How do you know?"

If they said something like, "Well, I'm a good person, so I believe God will let me in because I'm a good person," you would know that they are not saved, because they rely on their good works for salvation. Then you would share the Gospel with them.

I quickly implemented this method of evangelism. I led two people to the Lord in my high school. Then they shared their faith with others, and within 2 weeks we counted 70 boys that gave their lives over to Jesus!

Very soon we began to hold prayer meetings at the school. I was in a boarding school during weekdays at that time. We would meet behind a building, and pray fervently. These boys followed my example to pray passionately.

I remember a few other students walk by us one night, as we prayed in the dark, with just a little light a short distance away. We just kept praying. Later that night I was called to see the *koshuis-vader* – the boarding school father who was in charge.

He asked me, "So and so told me that you and a group of boys were behind such and such a building tonight. Is that true?"

Yes sir.

"And what were you doing there?"

We were praying, sir.

"Okay... And is it true that you were speaking in unknown tongues?"

Yes, sir.

"Okay... And is it true that at some point you were throwing someone up into the air?"

No, sir.

He then told us not to do this anymore, and at first, I said, "Yes, sir," but later continued it anyway. I got into a lot of trouble for this, but what can you do. We later prayed in the local church in town on Thursdays, when we were allowed to go to town between approximately 2-4 p.m.

Those were wonderful days, and I will always remember the wonderful work God did in the lives of those boys, and in my own life.

Bible college

Time came for me to graduate from high school, and I still did not know what I was going to do to prepare me for ministry. The Pentecostal church we attended had a 3-year Bible College program in Johannesburg, but I did not want to do this.

This was 1986, and there was a book out that proved that Jesus was going to return in 1988. If I went to Bible College, Jesus would have come before I even graduate, and there were a lot of souls to win before He returned!

Now, the evangelist I had talked about earlier also had a little ministry preparation course, but this on only was for 3 months. I felt very interested in doing this course, and then going out evangelizing.

But I did not have clear direction. However, God has a way. The Bible says, "A man's heart plans his way, But the LORD directs his steps" (Proverbs 16:9, NKJV.) God was watching out for me. God clearly led me to the *Berea Theological College*, where I completed my 3-year on-campus studies. This is how it happened:

It was December, 1986. South Africa's school years begin in January (not September, as in the USA,) and end at the end of the year. Think of it – I have one month before college starts, and I don't even know where I'm going to!

I was working on the resort that my dad had been managing now for several years. Once in a while I would swim and enjoy the resort amenities myself. As I was swimming in the hot pool, I met a very nice man. He told me, "So, I hear you want to be a preacher, and need to go to college?" This began the conversation. Back and forth we went as we discussed things related to college, the Lord, the Lord's return, etc. etc. It turns out he was actually a lecturer at *Berea Theological College*, which was the Bible College for the *Full Gospel Church of God* – South Africa's second largest Pentecostal denomination.

After our long talk, he said, "Now, normally you would have to come in for an interview at the college. But if you decide this college is for you, just consider this your interview!" After I eventually went to the college, and realized the college standards, I am still amazed that the lecturer and faculty approved the *pool-interview* to qualify as a real interview.

My years at *Berea* were pleasant ones. I made wonderful friends, with whom I am still friends with today.

My friends and I often went to the city of Pretoria, and preached on the streets.

After Bible college, when I entered the full-time credentialed ministry, I continued my studies by correspondence at UNISA – the University of South Africa, where I earned B.Th. status. Later in my life I would be awarded an honorary doctorate degree from the School of Bible Theology Seminary and University, and later earn a Doctor of Theology from the Trinity Graduate School of Apologetics and Theology. Using 12-point font, I personally typed out (not copying and pasting anything) 650 letter-size pages of coursework and thesis, which amounted to 277,087 words. My thesis was about *The Deity and Humanity of Jesus Christ*, available in my book, *Son of God and Man.* But let me share another story of my time at Berea…

The Sick begin to get healed

There was a little school for black Africans not too far from the College. I found out who the trustees were for the school, and asked if I could hold a week of meetings there.

The meetings were held in one of the classrooms, but I preached as if there were thousands of people there. We actually had a good attendance.

In one of the services, I asked if there was anyone deaf, in either one or both their ears. A young girl came up, and I prayed for her. Up to this point, I had never seen a deaf ear open with my prayers, but I prayed with boldness and authority, almost as if she definitively would be healed.

In the natural, I would be quite nervous, but *under the anointing* those fears were squelched. I prayed with all my heart, and then asked her if she could hear anything from that ear. To our amazement, she could hear!

Her father was there too, and we asked him about it. He confirmed that she had been deaf in that ear, and told us for how long.

I was elated! God had just done a wonderful miracle, and *He used me.* This was the beginning of greater things to come, but even then, miracles did not happen as frequently yet.

Chaplain

Like Israel, South Africa also required her citizens to serve in the army. We had to serve for two years once you turned 16. But if you are still in school, it can wait. And thereafter, if you go to college, army can wait too, but eventually you will have to do your military service.

Your college education would also help place you in an appropriate place in the army, e.g. doctors would serve in the Medical Corps, etc. Since I had just completed my Biblical studies, and had become licensed in the ministry, I was placed in chaplaincy.

At first, I was not too keen on doing my military service, but once we started, I began to enjoy the army very much.

Bootcamp however was quite tough. I think they made sure us would-be chaplains would never forget it. We were probably about 500 chaplains-to-be in bootcamp, most of the Dutch Reformed Church, and many others such as Baptists and Pentecostals. We even had two Jewish rabbis doing their fair share.

We had very little sleep, and seemed to drill and run all day long. And all-night reconnaissance, etc. After bootcamp, we began officer's training, which demanded much study, but much less drilling and running. I have to tell you a little story here.

The upper echelons decided that it was time to reward us all with a movie in another building on the camp. The last thing any of us wanted was a movie. We all would rather sleep. I don't know who it was, but one of our Pentecostal brethren came up with a great idea. He said that he had read somewhere in the rule book of our denomination that ministers of the Gospel may not smoke, drink, gamble, and ... watch movies!

I knew about smoking, drinking, and gambling, but I had never heard about movies. But we all as one man took our stand. One brother told the officer that we personally did not mind watching a movie, but that we were worried that we could get into trouble with our denomination if word reached them that we had watched a movie. Of course, this was all nonsense.

So, the officer went to consult with his superiors, and came back to us on the issue. "So, you cannot watch a movie because of your religious beliefs, correct?" Yes, someone agreed, and the rest of us just went with the flow.

"Okay, you do not have to go. So, the captain has decided that instead you will spend the next 3 hours polishing the floors, scrubbing the showers, and cleaning the toilets." After a moment of silence, I remember a brother next to me say, "Lieutenant can't be serious..." Another brother spoke up and suggested that we would rather opt to go watch the movie after all. But the damage was already done, and could not be reversed.

And off went the Calvinists to their movie, and us Pentecostals began scrubbing.

Abducted

I really did enjoy the army. At first, I was with *1 South African Infantry*, and then was moved to different places. One of the places I really liked was patrolling the border between South Africa, and our northern neighbors – Zimbabwe and Botswana. I often preached 5 times a day as I visited the troops patrolling the border. Those were great times.

When I got to that area at first, I was always staying in the officer's quarters, then driving out to the troops, and coming back to the officer's quarters by night. But I felt I wanted to stay in the bush with the troops. I talked to a couple of officers about it, and they were keen on the idea.

Some arrangements were made, and I was giving permission to do so. I was picked up by another private on the first night. As we drove to where the troops were stationed, a kudu ran ahead of our car. Soon after we saw two huge porcupines. I mean they were huge. This was the bushveld at its best. I was reminded of my colleague - another chaplain who would crawl up into a herd of buffalo, but I was not going to do this. There were also elephants, and we had to wisely maneuver our vehicle past them.

Finally, we arrived at a deserted place with one lightbulb in the middle of nowhere. The private told someone over his walkie-talkie that the pastor was there, told me they would be there for me soon, and drove off.

After he left, I felt very alone. I still had the kudu and porcupines in my head, and wondered what else might be in these bushes. I was also on the very Limpopo River that was our border with Zimbabwe, which was a communist country, and where many freedom fighters had committed many atrocities. The river was dried up too, and one could walk right across its sandy soil.

I decided to hide in the shade of a tree to hide myself from the light from that single lightbulb in the middle of nowhere. Suddenly, I saw a man walking down the dirt road, with a rifle in his hand. He was dressed in a military overall, but did not look like a South African soldier at all. His wooly hair was unkempt and puffy. He looked just like the terrorists I have seen in the documentary videos.

But he saw me. He pointed the rifle at me and said, "Lie down on the ground!" I could not believe it. There was no way I was going to lie on the ground. I knew I would get shot. He demanded that I lie on the ground again, with much anger in his voice. I told him I would not lie on the ground, and that he could do me no harm, because the angels of God are with me. He cocked his rifle, and said, "I don't want to hear about the church – you lie on the ground!"

Suddenly I saw several men come out of nowhere, running in our direction, with their faces covered. I did not know if they were there to help me or hurt me. In retrospect, I should have started swinging (I used to box as a child, and never lost a fight – all two of them.) But I was paralyzed with fear. Whoever those men were – they tackled me hard and brought me down to the ground. They put a sack over my head, bent my arm behind my back, and forced me to go with them.

They took me through bushes, scraped my head on the branches, some spoke Afrikaans, another Sotho or some other African language, and another German, and I knew that he must have been from the then socialist country of East Germany.

They took me to *the chief* who attempted to extract information from me. They held a live coal from a fire in my face, and I understood that I would be tortured by it. *The chief* asked me, "We want to know about the paratroopers. How many are there?" I knew I could not give them this information, and there was no way I would give out that information, even if I knew how many *parabats* there were. I answered them with an answer that was unrelated to what they asked. "I completed my studies in Pretoria."

"Give him some water! He is talking!" This went on for about 15 minutes. Questions about the troops, and getting unrelated answers from me.

Suddenly, they pulled the sack off my head. "Did you have a big fright, *Dominee?!* (i.e. Pastor?!) They all laughed. It was all a prank. Up to that point it never occurred to me that this might have been a prank. I had been totally stunned by fright, but now I was absolutely relieved!

We all had a good laugh about it, and I kept talking to them about it all night, and that I was so glad it was not real. I took the prank in good spirits, and had a great repour with them.

This was when I was with the paratroopers. But I have to tell you another humorous story. After ministering to the paratroopers, I was sent to 32 Battalion. "32" was one of the most notorious, feared, and controversial battalions in those days.

They were Portuguese-speaking Africans that fought alongside the South Africans against the communists in Angola. After the Angola conflict ended, they were repatriated to South Africa, and now served in the South African army.

They were led by South African officers. After I met the captain, he asked me if I could speak Portuguese, and if not, how would I be preaching to the troops? I said that I thought that perhaps they could provide me with a translator. He said that it could be arranged, but in the mean time I should know that the troops would be quite offended if they talked to me and I did not communicate with them. But according to the captain, all I had to say was, "Não fale m..." If I said this, the troops would know that I could not speak Portuguese.

They sent me to my tent that had been especially designated as the chaplain's quarters. A dear old soldier, his hair white with the frost of many winters, kindly carried my stuff, and made my bed for me. While he was doing his thing, I asked him, "Praat jy Afrikaans?" He shook his head and said *Não*. "Do you speak any English?" *Não*. So, I told him - no problem because, "Não fale m..." His eyes lit up in surprise, he shook his head and said something like, "*Ah-ah, Não- Não- Não.*" I was sure I didn't say it right, but apparently, I did.

I began to mingle with some of the other troops. The same story – I would ask if they could speak Afrikaans or English, they replied that they could not, or could only speak a little of it, and I would tell them, "Não fale m..., Não fale m..., Não fale m..." They all seemed to have the same reaction as the older gray-headed veteran.

That evening I met with the South African captain again. He asked me if I had settled in, etc., and I asked him what exactly those words were, and how to pronounce them correctly. He told me they were "Não fale m...," and that it meant, "Don't speak (the s-word.)"

Oh boy, here I am, the new chaplain in the bush, telling all the troops to not speak the s-word to me. Of course, I took the prank with a good attitude, but didn't use those words again. I never say a foul word.

However, when I preached my first sermon to 32 Battalion, I told the story of how I was pranked. It had a great effect. Oh, did they laugh. They took me in and made me feel welcome. Again, I had a great repour with them, and I preached the Gospel to them.

Before I went to do my military service, a prophetic minister told me that I would not do my full two years. He was right, because soon afterwards many political changes began to happen in South Africa, and I only did about 1 ½ years.

The army days were the good old days.

Going international

After the army, I began to travel as an evangelist. I had an uncle in the USA, John Hitchcock and my aunt Cornelia. They were evangelists, traveling in their motorhome, preaching the Gospel around the country.

Uncle John and Cornelia were very kind. They had their own needs, but at some of their services they had made mention about me, and received an offering for my air ticket.

I can tell you long, interesting stories here, but I cannot get into it too deep right now. But let it suffice to say that the Lord was at work. I must tell a couple of short stories though, because it shows how God works.

Firstly, when I was 14 years old, I had a dream that I was fishing with another minister in a place called *Bonn*. I did not even know there was such a place. I told my dad about it, and he told me that *Bonn* was the capital of West Germany at that time. That I was fishing with a minister mean that I was winning souls, for Jesus said we would be fishers of men. My dad said that he didn't know what to tell me, except that I should remember that dream.

Fast-forward several years. I'm done with my military service, and about to travel as an evangelist. I began to pray about what to do, and as I was praying, I suddenly sunk into a 2-second sleep. During those 2 seconds, I heard one word in my spirit, "Norway!" I instantly knew that I had to go to Norway.

So, when I began to travel in Europe, I head towards Norway. I did not know anybody there. All I knew was that I had a train ticket to anywhere in Europe. Then, I saw on my map that both

Frankfurt (Reinhard Bonnke's ministry headquarters,) and Bonn (the city I dreamt about) were on the way to Norway.

So, I first arrived unannounced at Reinhard Bonnke's headquarters in Frankfurt. I had never met Brother Reinhard, but I had watched his videos, and listened to his tapes over and over again. His ministry had greatly inspired me.

The staff told me that Reinhard Bonnke was not available at the time, but kindly showed me around the offices. "And this is Reinhard Bonnke's office." I looked at that chair, and the thought that Bonnke actually sat on that chair... Sheepishly I asked, "May I please touch it?" They said yes, and I touched the top of the backrest of the chair. I was amazed that this is where Reinhard Bonnke actually sat.

Later on, Bonnke's associate evangelist said to me, "So you have *never* met Reinhard? Let me see what I can do." Within 15 minutes, I heard that deep voice of Bonnke as he came down the stairs. And for 15 minutes I was talking face to face with the man of God. Everything he said felt prophetic to me.

When we said our goodbyes, I pulled out a small little paper, and asked him if I could have his autograph. Bonnke said, "I will give you something *bettah*," and handed me his book, *Evangelism by Fire*, and signed it for me, and we parted ways.

I was asked to do a devotion to their staff the next day, and that I could stay with their janitor that evening. After meeting with Bonnke, I went straight to a forest in the area, and spent an hour or two with the Lord there. I wrote down everything Bonnke told me in the back of that book he had given me.

When I arrived back at the janitor's quarters, he said to me, "Anni (Bonnke's wife) wants you to have dinner with them!" Wow, I could not believe it. That night, I spent that evening hours with Bonnke and his family. They had a large cherry tree in their back yard, and for 2 hours we ate cherries as we talked.

I cannot tell you how honored I felt. What a beautiful, precious family. And what an honor to spend this kind of time with one of my greatest heroes in the Lord.

But that was not all. Bonnke asked me where I was heading from there. I told him about Norway, and about my dream about Bonn. Bonnke told me that he knew a pastor in Bonn, picked up the phone, and I remember his words in German, and could understand the first sentence perfectly, "Ich habe hier einen jungen mann…" (I have here with me a young man…")

When Bonnke hung up, he turned to me and said that the pastor in Bonn was having an evangelistic outreach in Bonn that Saturday, and that I would be preaching. Wow. Well, I did preach in Bonn, and when I gave people an opportunity to accept Jesus, thirteen people raised their hands for salvation. My dream of when I was 14 had finally come to pass. I was 22.

God is so good! Then I head towards Norway. Long story made short, when I got to Norway, there was this one drunk, unkempt, and unshaven man with blood on his nose from a fall he had, keeping bothering me. "You must come to my house. There are many mountains, it is beautiful…" He wouldn't leave me alone. Finally, I just took his address to get him off my back, so that I could concentrate, and look at the map.

Finally, I just took the next train going north in Norway. I traveled from city to city, saw some beautiful sights, visited a church, gave my testimony there, then kept traveling north. When there were no more trains or busses to go any further north, I went east into Sweden, then further east into Finland, then all the way south to Helsinki, where I spent the entire day walking slowly through the city just praying and praying, mostly in tongues.

At the end of the day, I heard the voice of the Lord again. "Do you remember that drunk man? He was the one I sent to you! Tell him that he must accept Christ, and that I will use him." I made my way back on a train, and head to Norway, to the address he had given me. Within another day or two, I arrived at the doorstep of his beautiful home.

I knocked on the door, and his daughter opened. I told her the short story plainly, and she invited me in. After a few minutes the father came down. "Australia, right?" No, *South Africa*. "Oh, yes, I remember now." We sat down as they offered me some hospitality.

After a nice talk, he told me about people across the *fjord* (bay) that he knew that talked about God very much the same way I talked about Him. The next day I met with them and had a nice Bible study with them. They were so blessed and happy to have me. They just *had* to introduce me to their pastor, and by that Sunday I spoke in Norway's second largest Charismatic church!

Many years later, the pastor still told me that my visit there impacted his life.

All this came from a simple word I heard in South Africa, "Norway!" And through that word, I reached a lost soul, spoke in the second largest Charismatic church, and impacted their pastor's life.

Heidi

I must now tell you how I met and married my beautiful wife Heidi. This story begins with my visit at Reinhard Bonnke's home. I already told you about my meeting with him, and all the wonderful things the Lord made happen, but there is one more thing. Before I left, I told Bonnke that I would go to Bonn, then Norway, and then America, where I would join with my Uncle John.

Bonnke then told me, "The Holy Spirit told me that when you go to America, God is not only going to do something for your ministry, but He will also do something special for you *personally*." Little did I know that this *something personally* would be the greatest gift God gave me – her name is Heidi.

This is how it came about. When I arrived in America, my Uncle John and Aunt Cornelia Hitchcock picked me up. They were both from South Africa, and felt that God had led them to America, where they traveled with their Greyhound bus that they had converted into a motorhome.

Uncle John has an amazing testimony, which I want to insert here, because it is powerful. He had suffered from Meningitis when he was a child, which left him with a "stammering, stuttering tongue," as he puts it. He says that he had never met anyone ever that stuttered worse than he had. He could not even say his own name without a struggle.

Eventually he found Jesus, and joined his friends as they preached on the streets of Johannesburg. He would play the accordion, and they would preach. During a Pentecostal Revival, he received the baptism in the Holy Spirit, and spoke in tongues. He then switched to English, and discovered that he was completely fluent. "Is this me? Is this me?!" he exclaimed. But the next morning he stuttered again. He was so disappointed, but went to the Lord in prayer, and prayed fervently in other tongues. Suddenly, his tongue was unlocked, and he could speak in English and Afrikaans fluently again.

This became the pattern of his life. Before he preached, whether on the streets or in church revival services, he would first pray in tongues until "the anointing fell" on him. At that point he would be fluent, and preach. The only way he *could* preach was to do so "under the anointing."

God used him in mighty ways, but do yourself a favor and get his book on Amazon.

Anyhow, I joined them, and traveled with them on and off for 8 months. We traveled around, and made our way to Kentucky. After a while in Kentucky we hit the road again. I remember Uncle John stopping at a stoplight, and saying, "Lord, should we go north or south?" He felt God wanted him to go south, and we wound up in Tennessee and Texas, and preached in those areas.

In Dallas, Texas we met Dr. Ray Chamberlain, who pastored a church in Salisbury MD. He was in Dallas for a missions' conference, and was the head of their *Fellowship's* missions' department. A week later, I got a call from Brother Ray. He told me about this lovely young lady in his church, and that he told her about me, and suggested that perhaps we could correspond by mail.

Heidi said that she would *love* to have a *pen-pal* in Africa, and soon I received a letter from her. He picture was beautiful. She had won Ms. Delaware USA's *Ms. Photogenic* with that picture, and later was the second runner up in the Ms. Delaware USA beauty pageant.

Of course, I went back to South Africa soon, traveling first throughout Europe again, and also through Central Africa. In my letters I would tell Heidi that within a month I would be at such and such an address, and by the time I go to that destination, lo and behold, there would be a letter or two from Heidi.

We continued this pen-pal relationship for 3 years and 3 months. Though neither of us at first seriously thought we would ever meet, the more we corresponded, the more we felt that we should meet at least once.

The Lord had instructed me during that time *not* to leave South Africa's borders, except for Swaziland for about a week of ministry. But in October 1994, in the desert town of *Postmasburg* the word of the Lord came to me again. He told me that it was time to go back to America.

I called Heidi (who by this time was working for the Lester Sumrall Evangelistic Association in Hawaii, after she had graduated from Liberty University in Lynchburg VA,) and told her about my plans to come to the East Coast of the USA, and that if there was any chance to meet up, that would be great.

We had hardly ever spoken over the phone by that point, because international phone calls were so expensive in those days. Heidi told me that she had been praying about going back to the East Coast, and that this call was confirmation. She would go back to the East Coast whether or not we met each other at all.

Well, by February 1995 I flew to the USA. When I saw North America below from my airplane window, I heard the Lord say, "Welcome home, my son." At that point I wasn't sure what that meant.

I met Heidi on Tuesday, and went to Brother Ray's church with her and her parents that Sunday. During the praise and worship, I heard the voice of the Lord yet again within my spirit. He said, "My son, I brought you here to be part of the revival I am bringing to this country. And I am placing her by your side to be part of it."

Wow. On Monday we talked about our futures, as if we were going to get married. It just happened so naturally. We were engaged soon.

After a month or so on the East Coast, I departed for California, and preached in that area. It would be 3 months before I would see Heidi again, and throughout those 3 months all I could think of was Heidi.

I was afraid I would lose her. Every morning when I woke up, my heart would instantly beat fast in my chest. I could feel it physically. I had not heart issues or anything, but the stress of not being with Heidi, and the fear that I might lose her, caused my heart to beat wildly every morning when I woke up.

Those were three very long and hard months. But after three months, I made it back to the Maryland/Delaware area. I told Heidi I was still somewhere in Tennessee when I was actually almost back to the East Coast. When I knocked on her parents' door (where she was living), and came in, and she heard my voice downstairs, I will never forget how she rushed down the stairs towards me, and hugged and held me.

She definitely liked and loved me as much as I did her. I lived in a church in Georgetown, Delaware for the last few weeks before our marriage, and we were married not long after.

This was the *something personal* that God would do for me in America.

Marriage and honeymoon

We were married on June 3, 1995. But I first have to tell you a couple of stories about this.

Firstly, I had to ask for Heidi's hand from her father Mr. Ronald Souder. This was quite difficult. As for one, I could hardly understand what the man was saying. His mother could not speak English until she learnt it at age 6. Until then she could only speak *Pennsylvania Dutch* (i.e. *Pennsylvania Deutch/German.)* And although Mr. Souder spoke to me in English (he didn't know any Pennsylvania Dutch,) I remember him looking straight into my eyes and telling me something that sounded like it was very important, but I had no clue what he was saying. And I am sure my accent was hard for him to understand also! I saw a T-shirt that said something like, "Cool story bro, but I have no idea what you are saying."

But I had Heidi's mom Linda on my side, and she told me when a good time would be for me to ask him for Heidi's hand. One day she told me – tonight is the night. Everyone went to bed, and I waited for him in their living room. He was working shift work, and should have been home already, but it was 1 a.m. by the time he got home. "Oh, you're still awake," he said, and said goodnight and went upstairs to his room. I waited all that time nervously, just to hear him say that, and disappear.

I think I was actually relieved though. But Heidi's mom let me know a couple of days later when the right time would be for me to talk to Ronnie. The time finally came, and I told him a long story of how Heidi and I had been pen-pals for over 3 years, how we met, how this happened and that happened, etc. etc. and I finally got to my point and asked him if I could marry her. His response was short. "I just want Heidi to be happy." I took that as his blessing, and the rest is history.

Heidi's mom went all out on the wedding. When I say all out, I do not mean that they were throwing money everywhere. But every day Heidi's mom got something special for the wedding. She is an amazing administrator, which may explain why she was the executive director at the Manor House in Seaford for several years. She told me that the entire wedding cost them only $600. It was not that they were cheap or anything like that. The Lord just gave them so much favor, that when all was said and done, their out-of-pocket expenses were only $600. Praise God! Pastor Ray preached, and it was a beautiful wedding. My parents, Tony and Elaine, came all the way from South Africa for the wedding. My dad was my best man, and I am so thankful that they made the effort to be at our special day.

Even our honeymoon was a blessing! They had been friends with the owners of the *Boardwalk Plaza Hotel* in Rehoboth Beach, Delaware, who gave Heidi and I the *honeymoon-suite* for free for an entire week!

This hotel was so nice. When we got there, I was a little nervous to stay at such an expensive and luxurious place. We went to the grocery store first and bought bagels, bananas, and peanut butter, and some other things. It felt like we were smuggling these items into our room.

The bellman offered to carry our bags up to our room, and I did not know what to tip him. I told him he probably got much bigger tips than this, but I gave him what I thought was acceptable. Thankfully, he looked grateful for the tip, and off he went. I am just glad those bags didn't burst open, and our sin be revealed – the bagels, bananas, and peanut butter we felt we were smuggling into the room.

That whole week was great. We loved the beach, laid out in the sun a lot, and although we never went hungry, we were frugal with our spending. We ate the items we had brought into our room, and once a day we enjoyed the *early bird special* at the hotel's restaurant, or at some other place. We billed the hotel restaurant meals to our room, to pay it when we would check out at the end of the week.

Finally, it was time to check out. The front desk lady said we were all set, and that they were glad to have us, and to have a great day, and a safe trip home.

But she didn't say anything about our restaurant bill. So, I told her about it, that we billed our meals from the Victoria's Restaurant to the room…

"Oh no," she said, "All the meals were included in your stay!"

What?! If I had known that, I would have had the 12- or 16-ounce steak meals, not the 6-ounce with the 2 sticks of asparagus! And we would have gone to eat there more often!

Hahaha, it all worked out though. I have used this story as a sermon illustration about all the blessings that God's people are missing out on, because they don't know that they are entitled to these blessings. God's people are destroyed because of a lack of knowledge (Hosea 4:16.)

Revival services USA

Heidi and I began to travel together as evangelists. Those were great days with wonderful memories. We preached from church to church across the country. One trip from Delaware/Maryland to Mississippi felt especially long. It felt like the trip would never end. But we made it there, and had a wonderful revival.

In this context, the word *revival* in my dictionary means, "an awakening, in a church or community, of interest in and care for matters relating to personal religion; an evangelistic service or a series of services for the purpose of effecting a religious awakening."

It was so great to see people touched by God. Many people were saved (gave their lives to Jesus,) healed, delivered (from sinful habits or mental/emotional oppression,) and baptized with the Holy Spirit (experienced the power of God resulting in speaking in tongues.)

We would stay in people's homes – either the pastor's home, or at people from that church. It was such a blessing for people to open up their homes and privacy to accommodate traveling evangelists. We would talk a lot about God, and just life in general with our hosts, and I will always be grateful for their hospitality.

Having said that, it was also difficult at times. We did not have much privacy. And one day, we bought a *travel trailer*. This became our home. We would park the trailer next to the church where we were holding our revival, and plug into their electricity and water. Or at a trailer park, or at people's homes. Later we also stayed in hotels or motels.

There is no way I can tell of all the wonderful works that God had wrought in our revivals among the wonderful people of America. But I will share a story or two.

On one particular occasion, I was asked to preach on a Sunday morning and evening at a church in Baltimore. The services went well, and during the evening service the pastor asked me if I could continue through the week. That revival continued for three weeks – seven services per week.

The power of God seemed to be so strong in the meetings.

A rough looking lady told us that she was just walking past the church, when it seemed that something pulled her on her coat, and brought here into the meeting. She didn't even know it was church at first. She said she was on her way to get *another bottle.* She was addicted to alcohol. She said the devil was in her, that's how much she was tormented by the alcohol.

We prayed for her fervently, and you could see the Holy Spirit touch her. (Oftentimes the power of the Holy Spirit is manifested by people, shacking, trembling, suddenly weeping, experiencing supernatural heat, sometimes falling to the floor, laughing ecstatically, speaking in tongues, feeling as if electricity us running through their bodies, etc.)

The next night, a beautifully dressed lady came up for prayer. I had no idea who she was, but when I looked directly to her face as she stood before me for prayer, I realized she was the rough looking lady from the night before! I was amazed at the transformation. She was changed by Jesus on the inside and out!

There was another man – I remember his name was Danny. Danny had been sitting in those meetings night after night. At some point during the revival, he received his deliverance from crack cocaine, but none of us knew this. He kept it to himself, and just kept on coming to hear the Word, and receive from the Holy Spirit.

Suddenly, Danny came up to the front of the church with a determination to tell us what God had done. His testimony was something like this: "Last week God delivered me from crack cocaine, but I didn't feel confident enough to come up and tell you what happened. But tonight, I heard the right-side speaker (of the sound system) pop loud. I turned to the sound man, and wondered what he was doing, why he suddenly turned the right-side sound up so loud. Then I realized – it wasn't that he turned the right-side sound up, it was my deaf right ear that suddenly opened! This is what gave me the courage to come up here and tell what God has done for me!"

Talking about people experiencing the power of the Holy Spirit, I remember a very precious occasion at another church. There was this one little girl, probably about 9 years old, who came to the services. She was not even from that church, nobody knew much about her, except that she had many unfortunate family issues, and that she was struggling emotionally.

That little girl came night after night. She never smiled, she just sat there listening to the Word, and watching. Then, one evening, the Holy Spirit fell on us. Several people in the congregation began to laugh for joy. It popped like popcorn – first someone here, then someone there, and before you knew, people were laughing for joy all over the place.

Suddenly, the little girl got the joy. She laughed and laughed, and it was a beautiful sight. The meeting lasted for quite a long time, and people were touched by the Lord. Eventually, the meeting ended, and we dismissed the congregation.

I spent some time visiting with the people who wanted to talk, and encouraged them in the things of the Lord, etc. But out of the corner of my eye, I saw that little girl standing there patiently, giggling every so often. Then she would get quiet, and then the joy would burst forth again, and she would giggle and laugh.

I excused myself from the adult I was speaking to, so that I could talk to the little girl. I always make a special effort to make children feel important. "Hi, how are you? I am so glad the Lord touched you in such a wonderful way."

Sputtering her words through her laughter, she asked, "How do you make it stop?" I told her not to worry about it. Just receive what God is doing, and let Him complete the work. The laughing will end at some point, but it is wonderful what God is doing. Let Him just finish what He is doing.

Although this wonderful infilling of the Holy Spirit is wonderful and glorious, people often say that they laughed so hard, that their bellies hurt (because of the physical exertion that happens when you laugh like that.)

When we walked outside, I saw the little girl waling toward their car, still laughing. The last I saw of her was when she turned her head towards me as she was walking, and forced in another word, "Help!" Hahaha, it was so glorious and beautiful. She could not make the joy stop, and had to ask for help. I never saw that little girl again, but I always cherish what God had done in her. It would be so great to meet her again, and see what God had done in her life.

During another revival, God was really moving among us, and the people were revived and rejoicing. One man came forward for prayer, because he could hardly hear. After prayer, he could hear clearly! He said that it felt like to battleships collided in his ears, and they were instantly opened.

During another revival, we witnessed a powerful miracle. I prayed for a lady in here wheelchair. Not much seemed to happen, but I encouraged her to keep on believing God. I went back to the platform to doing other things, praying for others, etc. But suddenly, I felt a moment of glory. It was so strong and convincing, that I rushed to her in a hurry, prayed for her again – this time with strength and boldness that could only have come from God, and raised her up by faith.

She stood up! Then she began to walk up and down the altar (the area between the platform and the pews,) and when she realized what had happened, she dropped to her knees and made the sign of the cross.

When she got home, her daughter was amazed. No only could she walk, but she said that she even saw her mom have her bounce back.

Another revival in Pennsylvania was absolutely glorious. After one of the services, Heidi and I stopped at a gas station to buy a cup of tea to take to our motel room and enjoy there. I waited in the car while Heid went in to get it.

She took a little longer than usual, but she told me when she got back into the car that she invited the store clerk to the meetings. He told her that he had just bought a suit for a wedding, and was looking for an opportunity to wear it again, and that he would come. His name was Matt.

When another store associate came in for her shift, he told her that he was going to the revival. What?! Matt going to a revival? This she had to see, and decided to go with him. She told her friend Andy about this, and he and his brother decided to come also.

That next night, all four of them sat on the front row. At some point Matt left the meeting, and I felt very sad when he didn't come back – neither that night nor any of the other services. By that time, he had taken his jacket off, and his shirt was hanging out. I think it was the power of the Holy Spirit, and that he perhaps could not stand the conviction of the Spirit, calling him to repent of his sins. About a month later, we learnt that he was stabbed with a knife, and the pastor visited him in the hospital. I pray that by now, perhaps he had given his life over to Christ.

But back to the services. The other kid that came with Matt, whose name was Andy, really received from God. Andy received Jesus as his Lord and Savior, and when he was prayed for, he fell to the floor under the power of God, and testified about the power that surged through his body.

But that was not all. In another service, I prayed for his one ear that had been completely deaf. He could hear from that ear perfectly! I even had him stop up his other ear, then stand behind him, and asking him to repeat what I said. I went all the way to the back door of the church, and he could hear me perfectly.

Of course, we all rejoiced when God did such a wonderful miracle. But I did not realize the full extent of this miracle.

A few months later, I talked to the girl who had brought him to the service. She told me again how wonderful it was that Andy had received his hearing, and I rejoiced with her over the phone. But then she said, "But I don't think you realized what really happened. Andy went back to his doctor, and told him that he could hear. The doctor said it was impossible, because there was no eardrum in that ear. But Andy insisted that he could hear out of that ear now. So, the doctor checked him out, and found that he now indeed had an eardrum in that ear!"

How Andy got that eardrum, I do not know. Either the hearing specialists erroneously said that he had no eardrum in that ear, or God created one in that service!

To end this chapter, I have to say that I feel so thankful and humbled that the Lord used Heidi and I during those days of revivals (special meetings,) and revival (a move of God.) We were married on June 3, 1995, and the Brownsville Revival broke out on June 18, 1995, with Pastor John Fitzgerald and

Evangelist Steve Hill. Rodney Howard-Brown traveled the country, starting fires of revival wherever he went. Benny Hinn held great healing crusades all around the world.

When God said to me, "My son, I brought you here to be part of the revival I am bringing to this country. And I am placing her by your side to be part of it," He kept His word, and I was honored to be part of those days of revival.

However, I feel deep inside of me that God is not done. I feel that however great those days of revival were, that God can do so much greater. We have not yet seen the full extend of what God can do.

"Wilt thou not revive us again: that thy people may rejoice in thee?" (Isaiah 85:6, KJV.)

Vision for international crusades

I have shared with you the wonderful work of God during our revivals in the USA, and I now want to share with you about the great soul-winning crusades we held around the world, which happened simultaneously what we were doing at home.

Early on in my life, God gave me a love for mass crusade evangelism. As a youth, I said that one of the most beautiful sights was when thousands and thousands of people had their hands raised to God. I also admired photos of multitudes coming to Jesus, and pasted them in the inside covers of my Bible. In time, God would bring these dreams reality.

When Heidi and I got married, we soon put together a clear vision for our immediate future. We believed God together that within a year we would have a service with 5,000 in attendance, and within 5 years, 20,000.

I could not leave the country because my application for permanent residence in the United States was not yet approved. But once it was approved, Heidi and I went to Southern Africa, where we spent 11 months. I had raised money for a sound system, and shipped it to South Africa, which we would use when we got there.

My family loved Heidi, and we traveled all around South Africa, mostly preaching in Afrikaans churches. Heidi was learning Afrikaans slowly, and although she couldn't speak it, she began to understand much of it.

The same kind of things I shared with you about our revivals in the USA, also happened in South Africa. After one of our healing services, a pastor told another pastor that he saw things in that revival that he had never seen in his entire life. God was healing people, and He was on the move!

We began to use our sound system in crusades among the black African population in South Africa. In one of the crusades, 800 people indicated their decision for Jesus on a decision card, giving us their names and addresses. After that crusade, one of the local churches let us know they were completely filled with new believers who had given their lives to Jesus in the crusade.

It was in this crusade that a lady was brought to the meetings in a wheelbarrow, because she could not walk. They had outfitted the wheelbarrow with a cushion to support her back. After prayer, she stood up, and the crowd went wild with joy, for they knew God had done a wonderful miracle. However, I could not get her to walk. I rejoiced that she could stand (which she was not able to do before,) but I was quite unhappy that she could not walk. So, we just gave God the praise, and went on.

However, that next Sunday she showed up at that local church – this time not in a wheelbarrow, but with only a walking stick! I thought about this, and came to this conclusion. I think the Lord healed her to the point that she could stand on her own feet during the crusade, but the Lord healed her to the point where she could walk when the man of God had left town – this way everyone knew it was God, not the man, who had healed her, and God gets all the glory!

Another lady in the service looked very troubled. I asked here, "Mama, what do you need from Jesus?" (I say these words often when I pray for people.) She told me that she was being tormented by a spirit every night. She had murdered someone years ago, did her time in prison, but that the spirit of the murdered person came to her every night. It walked on the roof, came into her room, and beat her up.

So, what did I do? First, I wanted to make sure that she was a child of God. Because if you belong to Jesus, the devil has no right to you. I led her in a prayer of salvation, to receive Jesus, and confess Him as her Lord and Savior. After that, I told her that the spirit that came to torment her is not the spirit of the murdered person, because that person is no longer in this world – whether in body or as a ghost. "...it is appointed unto men once to die, but after this the judgment..." (Hebrews 9:27, KJV.)

Those spirits are none other than demon spirits, over whom Jesus conquered in His death on the cross and His resurrection from the dead, and if we belong to Jesus, the devil has no power over us.

Then I told her that the devil fears the blood of Jesus, because the devil was defeated when Jesus died on the cross, etc. So, I told her, "When the spirit comes to you again, point your finger to the area where it is, and say, 'Satan, the blood of Jesus is against you!'" I made her repeat it a few times, almost like I made her practice it.

Well, I saw her again in the crusade on another night, and asked her how it went. Sure enough, she said that she heard the steps of the spirit walking to her on the roof, as it always did. Fear came upon her, but then she remembered what she was supposed to do. She pointed her finger towards the area where she heard the spirit, and said, "Satan, the blood of Jesus is against you!" And what happened then? Well, when she said, "Satan..." the footsteps stopped. And when she said, "The blood of Jesus is against you!" the footsteps ran off in the opposite direction, and tormented her no more!

"The Spirit of the Lord God *is* upon Me, Because the Lord has anointed Me To preach good tidings to the poor; He has sent Me to heal the brokenhearted, To proclaim liberty to the captives, And the opening of the prison to *those who are* bound" (Isaiah 61:1, NKJV.)

God is so good. But the 800 souls were still a far cry from the 5,000 souls we wanted in a single service within a year, and 20,000 souls in a singles service within 5 years.

However, God would do so soon.

Heidi and I packed our car and trailer with our sound system, water purification system, and whatever we needed to go the Central Africa. In Zambia we arrived late at night, and stayed in a room with no windows, but all night long we could hear goats mating and fighting with each other. It was a long night, but we were thankful for a safe place to stay.

Once we were in Malawi, we would stay in villages in little mud huts that the pastors made available to us. However, we pitched our two-man tent within the huts, because it helped against mosquitoes, and we were concerned about the rats.

We would preach in churches, but our big goal was to hold big crusades. We used the trailer as our platform, with our sound system in the back seat of our car, the speakers next to the platform, and used two big PVC pipes as light poles, with three floodlights on each of them. All of this was powered by our little generator.

We also showed the *Jesus Film* on white sheet. When we turned the lights back on, there were often around 1,000 – 3,000 people standing there. I would then preach to them, and minister to the sick.

Then, in Blantyre in Malawi, we were to preach on a soccer field. But when the hosts heard that we were Pentecostal, they withdrew their approval for us to use the soccer field. We made another plan. There was a bus station nearby, and we set up our equipment there. After some singing it became dark enough for us to play the *Jesus Film*. All night long the busses dropped people coming back from work, etc. After the film ended, we turned the lights back on. To my amazement, there they were – thousands of souls! I asked the pastors how many people they thought there were, and the consensus was about 6,000. We had reached our goal of having 5,000 people in a single service within a year! Praise God!

Now, what about the 20,000 people we trusted God for in a single service within 5 years? God did that too, and this is how it happened.

I had been to India once, and loved the people (I just love any nation, really.) I had preached at a conference, but it felt like a crusade to me, because I preached salvation, healing, and prayed for the sick, and God did wonderful things.

But now I wanted to hold a big crusade. By this time, I was 32. I worked hard in raising funds for this crusade, because even though I was grateful for the offerings we received at churches in the United States, they often barely covered our base expenses, yet God somehow always came through for us with some miracle to pay our expenses – food, lodging, clothes, etc. Funding an entire crusade was added on top of these expenses, and the expenses were in a totally different level altogether.

The crusade costs would have been over $30,000, but with wise spending on the part of our crusade director, we were able to pay all the expenses for a little less than $20,000, plus my air ticket, etc. We paid for the stadium, for the sound system, for the platform, for the carpets for people to sit on, for some transport, for 50,000 *wall posters*, which were plastered all over the city, for 100,000 *hand bills*, and several billboards across the city. 300 taxis were paid to display a banner on the back, and several jeeps were outfitted with colorful hand-painted advertisement, and a P.A. system on the roof, advertising the meetings throughout the city.

I fasted for a long time before these meetings, and felt confident and strong in the Lord, especially with the revelation that I was to minister like Jesus would have ministered, for Jesus was within me, ministering to the multitudes. I will say more about that revelation in another chapter.

About 6,000 people arrived at the first service. Although I had preached to 6,000 people in Malawi, I was quite disappointed that only 6,000 people came to our first service in India. In Malawi it cost me nothing, and in India it cost me almost 20,000. But I looked past the crowd size, and ministered to the individuals, whom Jesus loved so much.

That night, God did wonderful miracles, and the word spread. The next night there was about 15,000 people, the following night 17,000, and on the last night, a massive crowd showed up. I asked the pastors from America who came to do a pastors' conference during day time of the crusade, how many people they thought there were. They estimated the crowd size at about 35,000. Praise God!

I had asked God for 20,000 people in a single meeting, and God gave me over 30,000!

My crusade director told me that they had gathered about 27,000 decision cards for follow up, and that his phone was ringing constantly. He told me they started 27 churches from those decision cards.

"Now to Him who is able to [carry out His purpose and] do superabundantly more than all that we dare ask or think [infinitely beyond our greatest prayers, hopes, or dreams], according to His power that is at work within us, to Him be the glory in the church and in Christ Jesus throughout all generations forever and ever. Amen" (Ephesians 3:20, AMP.)

Victory in big crusade setback

After that crusade in India, I became obsessed with holding such crusades. I became fixated with the idea that I could win a million souls to Jesus every year.

To do that, I was going to hold a crusade with 100,000 people in attendance in a single meeting, with that amount of people saved over the course of the crusade, and prove that I could do it. Then, I would want to hold such a crusade every month, which would put the number to over 1,000,000 salvations.

We decided to hold that 100,000-people crusade in India. I prayed a lot about this crusade. I raised money, and it would cost us more than our previous crusade. We decided to hold it in the largest city in that region – in Hyderabad, India.

All seemed to go well. The money came in, and when I arrived in Hyderabad, I could see that everything was done right. All over the place there were billboards advertising the crusade, thousands of wall-posters, and all the same things we did for our previous, greatly successful crusade.

That night, I was all prayed up, dressed up, and ready for my ride to the crusade. God was going to do great, great things. But nobody showed up to pick me up at the agreed time. But of course, *African time* happens in India too, so I was not too anxious. But by 8:30-ish, I decided to call someone.

On the other side of the call, I could hear a commotion going on. "Sir, we have problems here, sir!" What had happened is that a militant religious group showed up seemingly out of nowhere to march on the streets against the crusade. I understand there were about 200 of them. The police met with them, and told them that they would go cancel the crusade, and that they should go home. The police went up on the platform, made an announcement that the meeting was cancelled, and turned the sound system off.

I was told that there were about 10,000 people in attendance already, which by now I knew was a good amount of people on an opening night. But I could hear the saints pray and praise God in the midst of the commotion.

I looked out of my window, and heard the Holy Spirit tell me, "This is proof that I have won in this city." I didn't understand what that meant, but I knew that God was in charge.

The next day, my crusade director went to the authorities, but we had another setback. Not only was the crusade cancelled, but there would be no pastors' conference either. He even went to the chief minister of the state, who gave him no audience.

He then went to court. The attorney wanted to charge us $10,000, but he explained that we did not have that kind of money, and they agreed on $2,000.

I was told to stay out of sight, due to the sensitivity of the case. I read about myself in the newspaper, and heard people in the hotel talk about it, who had no idea who I was. I heard one tell the other in English, "Did you hear what they did to the Christians?!"

My cameraman (an Indian) also interviewed the leaders of the militant religious group, without them knowing who he was. They probably thought he was just one of the press. They made no secret about it. They said that they were glad the police closed the meeting, because if it had continued, they would have sent their young men into the crowd, and that it would be terrible. Another one said that those Christians force people to convert (which is not true.) They also said that those Christians say that their gods were false gods, etc. However, when I preach, I do not preach against their gods. I preach about my Jesus, and make it clear that He is the only true God, without singling out their gods.

Christians told us about their persecution. One of them told us how that the militants entered into their church and beat up several of their people. Another told us how that she was kicked, even though she was pregnant, and had been bleeding since that time till now.

In the meantime, all we could do was hope and pray for the court case. The attorney was on fire. Though he was a Hindu, he asked the court, "Isn't India a secular nation? Doesn't our constitution secure freedom of worship for all religions?" It was amazing that our case was actually brought before the court that quick, because typically it could take months, maybe years to complete.

The judge made his decision. He ruled in our favor, and ordered that the crusade could continue. He also ordered that the police would protect us.

We rescheduled the crusade for the next week. When I went to the platform, I felt that a bullet might hit me at any moment, but woe to me if I preach not the Gospel (1 Corinthians 9:15,) and, "For whoever desires to save his life will lose it, but whoever loses his life for My sake will find it" (Matthew 16:25, NKJV.) Though we should wise, we should never deny the Lord, or shy away from spreading the Gospel, regardless of anything.

Well, the meeting went well, but we did not have more than 500 in attendance. Still, several people made a decision for Jesus, several were healed, and the Kingdom of God advanced.

So, where is the victory in all this? I was told by the local Christians that their *prestige* was raised because we won that court case. And that a precedent was now set that protected the Christians. In the past many of their cries for justice were ignored, but this court case changed things.

Soon afterward, I heard of other evangelists that held meetings in that area, which were very successful. I believe that our victory in the court paved the way for others to hold their meetings.

Perhaps hundreds of thousands or more have come into the Kingdom through other people's crusades because of our court case. And that's wonderful. Christ is preached, souls are saved, and the Kingdom of God keeps advancing.

Largest crowds

God is a God who makes dreams come true. He also allows setbacks that are just part and parcel of evangelism. He keeps us humble, with or without setbacks, and often does things in different and greater ways than we anticipated. God gave me an opportunity to speak to a half million people. Let me tell you how this happened.

I have not yet held my own crusade with 100,000 people in attendance in a single meeting, but according to my calculations, we had about 100,000 people in *combined attendance* in one of our crusades.

An American pastor and friend of mine said that when I got up to preach, God told him, "This is what I called him for." He also told me that he compared the crowd to a certain section of the *Orioles Stadium*, which seated about 50,000 people in that section. So, we estimated our crowd in India at about 40,000-

50,000 on that one night, and combined with the other nights, at about 100,000.

Since then, I am no longer putting out numbers, because it is possible to overstate the numbers, and it's not about the numbers anyway. I now just publish a picture of the crowd, and let people decide for themselves how many people were in the meeting. I rather focus on the souls that were saved, and the miracles God did.

Before I tell you about the half million people, let me tell you about this pastor who had gone with me to India – the one that compared the crowd size to the crowd in the *Orioles Stadium*. On this crusade, it was just him and me on the team. After our first night at the hotel, he came to see me in the morning. He told me that he had had kidney stones before, so he knows when one is coming on, and he was feeling that onset of a kidney stone. Now, there was probably some clinic in that area, but a hospital was far away. He asked me to pray for him about that kidney stone.

We joined together in prayer. We prayed a prayer of faith, believing that God would answer our prayer. I prayed over him passionately, for "...the effectual, fervent prayer of the righteous availeth much" (James 5:16, KJV,) or as the Amplified Bible puts it, "The heartfelt *and* persistent prayer of a righteous man (believer) can accomplish much [when put into action and made effective by God—it is dynamic and can have tremendous power]."

My brother received his answer to prayer by faith, and had no problems with kidney stones – not in that crusade, nor ever in his life. I talked to him this year, perhaps about 15 years after that prayer, and he has still not had another kidney stone issue. To God be the glory! Hallelujah!

Now, let me tell you about that half million people. I had asked Reinhard Bonnke if I could join them on a crusade, and was granted permission. It was wonderful. I sat with Reinhard

Bonnke every day, at every meal. And at 5 a.m. he did a devotion for his team.

When I arrived at the first night of the crusade, the saints of God were praying on that field. My eyes became moist, just watching them pray – thousands of believers, praying for God to move in their city, and to bring multitudes of unbelievers into the Kingdom of God.

God worked mightily. Thousands upon thousands of souls were saved, healed, and baptized with the Holy Spirit.

I asked Bonnke's right hand man, to show me how he counted the crowd. He called me over when it was the right time, and walked around and in the crowd with a diagram. He counted the people per square meter, in certain areas. He knew how many meters there were between one light pole and the next. Between other light poles the crowd was less dense per square meter, and noted that on his diagram. After a good 30 minutes or more, he determined that crowd size to be 500,000.

One night, Evangelist Reinhard Bonnke told me, "I want you to speak to the crowd on Saturday night." Saturday night came, and they introduced me. I spoke to the crowd about "Experiencing Jesus." At some point I encouraged them to shout His Name – JESUS! I said, "Who is your Savior?" JESUS! "Who is your healer?" JESUS! "Who will provide for you?" JESUS! "Shout His Name again!" JESUS, JESUS, JESUS!!!

There were a half million people in that meeting. Though it was not *my* crusade, it was an honor and a joy to minister to that massive crowd. It also did something in me. I know that God can do more than I can imagine.

Though I never had my own meeting with 100,000 people in attendance, God still did more than I could ask or think, and I spoke to a crowd 5 times as big!

That video is available on YouTube. Just search for "Joel Hitchcock Experiencing Jesus" and it should pop up. Its at https://www.youtube.com/watch?v=L-n3-3etI7w ...

Financial victory

One of the things that I have struggled with was financial victory. Even as I write these words, I can say that although God does indeed meet in all our needs, I have not yet seen the financial breakthrough that I know is possible.

To illustrate, I would go on a crusade, and spend like $20,000 on that crusade. Then I would return home, and literally be challenged on how to pay for my lodging, or even for food. Somebody might wonder why we didn't just use part of the $20,000 for our personal needs, and the answer is that I had raised that money *for the crusade,* not for other expenses, not even general ministry expenses.

Don't get me wrong, because God always took care of us, and I have never gone without. But the fact of the matter is that it has always been a struggle.

Sometimes I think of all the money we put into crusades, and I realize that with that money I could have paid our home mortgage off by now. I would have liked to have paid it off earlier to save on the interest, but we're just doing what we can.

Having said that, I have to tell you a couple of stories of how the Lord provided for us. I already told you how He provided for Heidi and my honeymoon, but let me tell you how he provided us with a car.

Actually, He provided for us on several occasions, but I'll just pick one of the car-provision stories for this purpose. When Heidi and I went to Southern Africa for 11 months, we bought a half beat-up VW Passat. In South Africa there is a joke about Passats – *Pas gekoop, en Sat gery* (Just bought, and already ruined driving it.)

Actually, the car was not too bad. But I knew something was wrong when we arrived home, turned the car key to the off-position, removed the key, and the car was still running! I had to put it in gear, hold my foot on the brake, and smother it. With this *faith-car* we held a revival in Alberton, Johannesburg. Again, the car broke down on the highway on a wet and cold day.

I walked to a random house and asked if I could call the pastor. He sent some brothers to help me, towing the car with a little Datsun/Nissan. At the pastor's house one brother said that the wiring was all messed up. He fixed it, and another brother donated a new battery. All this only 2 weeks before Heidi and I would go into Central Africa with it. Praise God for the family of God!

A week or so later, one of the brothers called me. He asked about my car, and I told him it was running better than ever. He was glad, but had a proposal for me. He said he was selling his car, and told me about it. He had been the only owner, it was not an old car, the air conditioning worked, had low miles, etc., etc. I knew there was no way I could afford this car, whatever he was going to sell it for. Then he said, "You probably would like to know the price?" Yes, what's the price? "One Rand," i.e. One South African Dollar, which was probably about 25 American cents.

Praise God! We drove out to "purchase" the car, took it to my parents' home, applied for our tags (which take much longer in Africa than it does in America,) packed it with our goodies for our trip to Central Africa – trailer and all, found out that the tags would be there on a certain day, got there at almost the moment the truck came to deliver the tags, attached the tags, and went straight from there towards Zimbabwe on our way to Central Africa!

God did a miracle for us, and though He was not early, He was not late, and right on time.

On another occasion, Heidi and I and our four kids were traveling across the United States with our travel trailer, preaching the Gospel. We preached in Texas, New Mexico, California, Oklahoma, and North Carolina, all in one trip, which lasted 8 months.

In Texas, a brother bought me a matching shirt and tie, but it was in Albuquerque, New Mexico that I put it on for the first time, a week or two later. As I put in on, I felt so good – you always feel good in something new. Then I prayed a prayer I had never prayed in my life, just a short, fleeting prayer, "Lord, provide for us that we can buy Heidi some nice clothes."

Off we went to the church, and I preached my heart out. The pastor wanted to know where I got the energy, because I was all over the place. He graciously received an offering for us, and was about to dismiss the meeting after a song, when he said, "You know, I feel I want to do something extra for the Hitchcocks. I know you already gave an offering to them, but I want us to receive another offering – one specifically for Sister Heidi, for her to buy her a nice outfit."

I was blown away! Never in my life had I asked God for money for clothes for Heidi. And never ever had anybody received an offering specifically for Heidi's clothes, and it all happened within about 2 hours from the point I prayed that casual prayer, to when it was answered!

While we were thankful for the money for Heidi's clothes, it was a double blessing, because I realized (again) that God actually hears us when we pray, and He answers prayer! I think this realization was the greater blessing!

When I was about to turn 30, we went to Rodney Howard-Brown's meetings. The meetings were powerful, and very blessed. Rodney called me up and ministered to me. He said God told him something, and spoke over me in Afrikaans, "'n nuwe begin..." (a new beginning.) I didn't laugh for joy at that moment, as is common in his meetings. I just received from the Lord. However, I did receive an outburst of joy in the other meetings. On Saturday, Heidi and I were sitting way in the back, because she had to have her feet propped up, being in the late stages of her pregnancy with our first child.

Rodney received an offering after he had taught a powerful message on stewardship. People began to give joyfully to the Lord, shouting praises as they did. Suddenly, Rodney looked right at Heidi and I way in the back. "Joel, you and your wife, come up here." When we got up there, he said, "Firstly, I am going to give you $1,000. But this is what God told me – He is going to give you a *big* financial breakthrough!" With that, he laid hands on us, both of us fell down under the power of God, laughing with joy, in the Spirit."

Then someone shouted, "It's his birthday." What? "It's his birthday!" Rodney then said, "Well, happy birthday! Someone just threw $5 on you." Then the entire church got up and started to throw money on us. The ushers even gave us the offering bucket. That day we went home with over $2,000.

Praise God! But that's not the rest of the story. We joined Rodney in that same month in Texas. During this revival of his, Heidi and I gave a very special offering. It was the largest offering we had ever given. Then I realized that part of the *financial breakthrough* was not so much the receiving part, but the giving part.

Giving the largest offering we had ever given was followed that same month with the largest income our ministry had ever had. Typically, Decembers were slow months for us, because we didn't preach much in December, because churches typically did not have evangelists in December. Yet God made a way to provide for us with more money in that month than at any other month up to that time.

I have to tell you of another wonderful provision from the Lord – this time not for the ministry, but for us personally. A couple of years ago, a dear lady asked to see us, because she had *something* for us. When we met with her, she gave us a check of $30,000! Wow, this has never happened to us. God had provided similar amounts in the past for ministry and crusades, but this was for us personally!

We immediately paid off some debts, and had nothing left, but felt elated that those debts were paid, and that God had provided for us personally.

It is wonderful to know the Lord not only takes care of His Kingdom's interests, but also for His servants, especially since we are His kids. We are *King's kids!* Thank You Jesus.

Pastoring a church

I had always been asked by people, "Do you think you would ever pastor a church?" I developed a standard answer, "Well, if God wants it, I would do it, but for now I feel we must just continue traveling as evangelists," and that is exactly what we would do.

But one day, a dear prophetic minister asked us if Heidi and I would like to have lunch after the service. During lunch he told us that he felt to tell us something, but didn't want to prophesy it to us, but rather just talk about it over lunch. He popped the question, and I gave him the standard answer. But the more we talked about it, the more I began to think that at least I should pray seriously about this.

For the next 3-4 months I prayed and prayed about it, and could not get an answer. It was so hard. Firstly, does God want me to pastor? Secondly, where would it be at? Colorado, South Africa, New Zealand? I literally considered these places. And if it was in my area where I lived, what would the local pastors say?

I began to call every pastor in the region that I had a relationship with, and they all gave me their full blessing. One even sent me $1,000. I felt that it was important for me to get the blessing from the local pastors. We decided to start the church in our home area – Sussex County, Delaware.

Did God *tell* me to start and pastor a church? Well, yes and no. No, He did not explicitly *tell* me as clear as in some other instances. But neither did I hear Him tell me *not* to start and pastor a church. What I can say is that I *felt led* to start the church. Sometimes God speaks clearly, and other times He *leads* you, and you follow His promptings in your spirit.

With no people and no money, we started the church. We called it *River City Church* – after Psalm 46:4, "There is a river whose streams make glad the city of God, the holy place where the Most High dwells" (Psalm 46:4, NIV.) *River* referred to the Holy Spirit (John 7:37-39,) and *City* to the Church of Jesus Christ, and our daily lives (Hebrews 12:22.)

Our first service was well attended, and we were off to a good start. But most people who came, just came to wish us well, or were perhaps curious, and didn't stay with us. The ones that did stay with us were a mix of people who really wanted to support us, and others had their own ideas of how the church should be.

I look back and remember the glorious moments we had in the services. People were saved, healed, and touched by God in a wonderful way. I was still an evangelist, and a revivalist, but in a pastoral position. And I loved it.

We did not have our own building, so we rented a place, but had to move to another place, and then to another, and another, all because of reasons mostly out of our control.

If I could do it over, I would do things different. I would make sure I had people and money before I start. But then again, if I could have, I would have. I would have a team and some important things in place to successfully launch the church.

During all this time, I continued to function in my calling as an evangelist. No, I would not be speaking as a guest speaker at different churches, but our own services were very evangelistic, mixed with pastoral care, and in-depth teaching of God's Word.

I also continued to hold international crusades, and held two of our largest crusades during those years. But I always put our little flock's needs first. I was not going to be their pastor, and never be there for them. As occasion presented itself, I visited them at their homes, or at the hospital, and loved our little flock.

Another blessing that the church proved to be is that I was home with my children during a very key period of their lives. My oldest son and daughter were 14 and 12 when we started the church, and my younger children grew up in our church. I am thankful that I could be with them during this time.

After almost 9 years this beautiful season of pastoring came to an end.

Our children

I am a family man. I love my wife and kids. They are everything to me. God has blessed me with four precious children. As I write this, I cannot believe how fast they grew up.

I once met Evangelist Steve Hill, who for some reason told me to always put my children first, and spend much time with them.

He said that they had done so, and all his children were serving the Lord, and that they were in the ministry with him.

I can thankfully say that I did this. I cannot tell you how many long baseball games, soccer games, and basketball games I attended to support my boys. And I have only one daughter, and am obviously very protective about her, and just want the best for her. I supported her ballet, lacrosse, softball, and cross-country, etc.

Anthony

My first child, Anthony, was born in 1999. With his birth, everything changed. I was holding a revival in Crisfield MD when he was born. I was relieved from my responsibility preaching that night, and could be with Heidi during the birth. I was back in the pulpit the next night.

I clearly remember the first time he smiled at me. And when He was just a couple of months old, while I was holding him during the praise and worship service, he locked eyes with me and went on a kissing spree. He kissed me all over my mouth and face. What a precious moment that was.

As he grew, I tried to do special things with him. I bought lots of cheap toys, buried them in the woods, and made a treasure map of where they were located. With his little backpack and lunchbox, we went treasure hunting. There was a huge fallen tree on which we sat. Today the remnants of that tree are barely visible, but I pinpointed it out to him just the other day.

He was the scholar-athlete at his school, and went on to play soccer at college.

Rebekah

Rebekah is my only daughter, born in 2001. I nicknamed her *Princess,* and *Sweetness.* She had a faint red birthmark on her forehead, and when she cried or was mad, it became more pronounced. We thought it might even be with her all her life, but it gradually faded away.

She had the cutest smile. She would crawl on the floor, stop, and look up at us. I would say with a higher pitched voice, "I see you!" Then she would smile brightly, and keep going. This happened more times than I can count.

When we went to the beach, she did not want the sand to touch her feet. If I lowered her closer to the sand, she would lift her feet, or pull them to the side. She definitely did not want sand on her feet.

I loved to hold her in my arms (like I did her brothers) during praise and worship. Someone came up to me and told me she always remembers the comfort she felt when her father held her like that.

One of our games was for her to run to me, and I would catch her. Then I would spin her around and around. She even bounced off the trampoline, diving towards me, fully assured that Daddy would catch her.

When we watched a movie, and anything would be remotely scary, she would crawl right up to me and sit here by Daddy, where it's safe. When she did ballet, she was so precious. At some point she lost interest in ballet, but those were good memories.

She would also get on my back in a pool, and we would play *Dolphie.* I would come up out of the water with her on my back, then down to the floor again, and back up out of the water like a dolphin.

For some reason, I cannot remember if we did the treasure map thing, but I'm sure we must have done that too.

During our church meetings, she would read the Bible for me, and at times join me in the platform, laying hands on those I prayed from. I have pictures of this, and they are some of my most precious memories.

She is very smart, studies hard, and earns really good grades like her older brother.

Timothy

When Timothy was born (2005), I shed a tear, but it didn't just gently stream down my cheek, it actually squirted out that moment he took his first breath, and cried his baby cry.

He had a perfect Apgar score, but by the next morning the doctors realized something was wrong. For over a week he hung between life and death at the A.I. Dupont Hospital. I am so thankful to that institution. Eventually he had surgery, and recovered completely.

I cannot describe to you the intense prayer and concern we had for Timothy. We completely gave him to the Lord. When Reinhard Bonnke saw him the first time, he said, "Little Evangelist!"

Like with his older siblings, I also made a treasure map for him, and we looked for those toys in the woods.

He became quite a little ballplayer, and his coaches and peers just loved him. His Little League team won the Delaware state championships twice in a row, sending them to Regionals, where they lost, but were *that close* to heading to World Series.

Timothy worked hard like his older siblings, and was able to buy his own car with his own money when he turned 16.

Like his older brother and sister, he is also very smart, and earns great grades.

Trey

Our youngest son Trey was born in 2007. He too has been such a joy. He had this little stuffed animal toy that played the *Walking in a winter wonderland* song. Trey was only 2, and would dance with the music, wiggling his hips.

When he was about 4 or 5, he did something special, and God honored it. I had a neck pain so bad that I could not move it at all. As I twitched my face in pain, Trey asked me what was wrong. After I told him, he said, "Daddy, Jesus heal you, me pray for you." He laid his hand on me and said, "Be healed, in Jesus' Name!" I was so blessed by this, and told Trey thank you, and I receive it. I did not give my pain another thought, went to bed, and woke up the next morning with zero pain in my neck! The regional administrative bishop of the Church of God in our area read about it on my Facebook post, and announced it at the camp meeting, where hundreds of people were blessed by that testimony.

Trey also became quite a ball player, and his team also won the Delaware state championship, and competed at the regionals. Trey developed an interest in making money. He would buy discounted items at Walmart, or at some other place, and sell them for a profit.

Although this memory is also quite faded in my mind, I know I also made the treasure map for him, to find toys in the woods, and having lunch on our little trip, as I also did for Anthony, Timothy and Rebekah.

Like his older brothers, he also helped a lot setting up the sound system and chairs on occasions.

All my kids have done so well in school. Their grades have been outstanding. I pray for them every single day of their lives.

When they were younger, I would lay hands on them every day, typically when they were in bed. I would speak a blessing over them, borrowing from Deuteronomy 28 and Psalm 1. I would say, "You are the head and not the tail, above only and not beneath. You are blessed in the city, and blessed in the field. Your enemies come against you one way, and flee from you seven ways. Everything you shall prosper."

We would also have devotions every day. We read the entire Bible through together, from Genesis to Revelation, and then began with Genesis again, but soon switched to reading devotionals. These were some of the greatest times with our children.

It is my prayer that they will all have happy lives, serve the Lord, be blessed with wonderful spouses and children, and be successful in their lives, as they pursue God's purpose for them.

"I have no greater joy than to hear that my children walk in truth" (3 John 1:4, NKJV.)

"Their children will be mighty in the land; the generation of the upright will be blessed" (Psalm 112:2, NIV.)

God delivers me from a dark season

It came out of nowhere, but maybe it was a long time coming.

I would wake up in the middle of the night with great anxiety – something very unlike me, because I know in whom I believe. In the dark, I would pace the room up and down as I prayed to my God. But it felt like I was forsaken by both God and man.

I told the Lord, "Lord, I know you have not forsaken me, but it feels like it." I really knew that God had not forsaken me, but wherever I looked, I could not see God. One night I read half the book of Job. Oddly, it was Job's struggles that encouraged me. I am a faith preacher, always positive, and standing on the Word. But when I read about Job, it felt comforting to me that I was not the only one that felt deserted.

Verses like this spoke to me: "So I have been allotted months of futility, And wearisome nights have been appointed to me. When I lie down, I say, 'When shall I arise, And the night be ended?' For I have had my fill of tossing till dawn" (Job 7:1-4, NKJV.) And, "My days are swifter than a weaver's shuttle, And are spent without hope. Oh, remember that my life is a breath! My eye will never again see good" (verse 6-7.)

Job felt that he would "never again see good." It literally felt like that to me. I felt deserted by both God and man. But God had not deserted me, it just felt like it. And let me tell you, thank God for a good woman. Thank God for Heidi. Heidi was so encouraging. She was strong, and has stood with me all the time.

I read the rest of Job on another night, and saw that the same Job who said that his eye would never again see good, had an encounter with God, and said, "I have heard of You by the hearing of the ear, But now my eye sees You" (Job 42:5.) He who thought he would not ever see good again, saw something better – he saw God!

I didn't see God visibly, but surely, I did see Him come deliver me. I also read Ecclesiastes, and then the Song of Solomon. During my read of the Song of Solomon, I felt my intimacy with God being renewed. By the end of the year, and in the beginning of the next year, something broke, and I was delivered!

One day I stood in our house, and felt a heaviness come upon me. I began to think how wonderful it would have been if a man of God called me out of the blue with a word of hope from the

Lord. I thought, "Lord, let a man of God call me and tell me God has not forgotten me, God has not forsaken me, and everything is going to be all right."

Then I changed my thinking. I thought of others that would also have wanted a man of God bless them with such a message. I said, "Lord, let *me* be the one to give hope to somebody today. Let *me* contact someone and tell them that God had not forsaken them, nor forgotten about them, and that everything is going to be okay."

Suddenly I thought of a certain man. I tried to remember his name, but it would not come to me. It had been about 20 years since we had last had contact. He had been a pastor, and I had held a revival for him at his church. I knew his church had closed, and that he had suffered several setbacks. But I just could not remember his name, nor even the town he had pastored. I did remember the state though.

Then I said, "Lord, let *him* contact me, and I will then give him this message." This was on Tuesday. On Thursday I saw a message from someone on Facebook Messenger. "Brother Joel, this is [*his name*] from [*his town*]..."

Wow! That was him! I looked at the dates again, and saw that he had contacted me the very day after I had prayed that he would.

Oh, did we have a blessed time over the phone when I called him. I encouraged him in the Lord, and he received it. And I was encouraged by the fact that the Lord heard my prayer. *Why* would I pray that this specific man would contact *me* so that I would encourage *him* with this message, and why would he contact me the very day after I prayed that prayer? Consider that we had not talked in years.

God is so good! He has not forgotten you or me.

Soon after this deliverance, I wrote the book, *Thank You God!* It was about the principle of thanking God in and for everything. I also wrote *Divine Romance* based on the Song of Solomon, about our intimacy with God.

If you ever go through a tough time, so tough that it seems you will never get out of it, hold fast. Keep your faith and trust in God. Even when it feels He has forsaken you, please know that He will never leave you nor forsake you. Hang in there. God is on the way, and your breakthrough will surely come.

Books

With God's help I have written several books. I would like to make this part of my testimony.

One Almighty Mediator was my first booklet I wrote. It is about Jesus being the mediator between God and man, because He *is* both God and Man. I no longer had a copy of this book, but over 20 years later, someone showed it to me. I was amazed that someone still had a copy. I duplicated it, and made some minor changes. Almost 70 pages.

The Great King and the Little Ant was written on the airplane on my way back from a crusade in India. It is an illustration of how God reaches us, like a great king would stoop low and reach a little ant. It is almost 50 pages.

When Jesus moves into your house is another illustrative story of what happens when you surrender your entire life to Jesus. Also, about 50 pages.

Young Fire – End Time Youth Evangelists for the Great Awakening was originally under another title – *The End Time Revival and Great Awakening*. It was one of my earlier books, which I wrote as a youth, and after looking at it again, I made some changes both in the title and content, to encourage younger people to be revivalists to reach their generation for Jesus. It is also filled with stories upon stories of the historical moves of God, revivals and the great awakenings. 150 pages.

Praying and Proclaiming God's Abundant Provision is filled with prayers with words directly from the Scriptures, that deal with financial and material provision, success, abundance, and prosperity. It is powerful, because it is based on direct quotes from the Bible. Over 100 pages. People have told me that they read it every day, and that it inspires them to prosper. The same title is also available specifically for women.

The Miracle Ministry, Signs and Wonders is about the supernatural element of Christianity, that God still does miracles, and healing. Almost 120 pages.

Harvesting Multitudes into the Kingdom is about evangelism, specifically massive evangelistic campaigns. 100 pages.

Miracles for the Multitudes is a combination of the above two books into one volume. Evangelist Daniel Kolenda graciously wrote the forward.

Your Daughters shall Prophesy is about Women's Ministry in teaching, preaching, and leadership. What began as what I thought would be a booklet, turned out to be a 160-page book.

Christ in You is about my revelation of our oneness with Christ, that He dwells within us, and that we become like Him. Reinhard Bonnke wrote the forward to this book. 300 pages.

Son of God and Man is about the deity and humanity of Jesus Christ. This was part of my doctoral thesis, and a topic that I am passionate about. Over 200 pages.

Divine Romance is about our intimacy with our Heavenly Bridegroom – Jesus Christ. It is based on the Song of Solomon. Over 140 pages.

Thank You God is about giving thanks to God in everything and for all things. Over 120 pages.

Divine Healing Prayer is several prayers for healing, based on Bible verses, so you pray the Word back to God. 50 pages.

Jehovah Incarnate is about Jesus Christ being God in the Flesh. This book took my 12 years to complete. I am so blessed by this book. It starts with God's "journey" in eternity, before anything else existed, to when He created everything, eventually becoming incarnate in His only begotten Son, when Jehovah God called Himself *Jesus*, and all about His life, death, resurrection, ascension, enthronement, the Holy Spirit, and Jesus' literal and bodily coming. 200 pages.

Tangible Healing Power is about the power of God that heals the sick, and filled with many testimonies of healing miracles that God did in our ministry. 120 pages.

All these books are available on Amazon, or at https://joelhitchcock.blogspot.com/p/products.html with links to Amazon etc.

Christ in You

When I was a teenager, I discovered this verse in the Bible: "And whatever you do in word or deed, *do* all in the name of the Lord Jesus, giving thanks to God the Father through Him" (Colossians 3:17, NKJV.)

I thought and prayed about what exactly this meant. I read that to do something in the name of someone meant that you had received power of attorney from that person, and that you would act on that person's behalf.

It meant that you would do something *as if* you were that person, for you are representing him.

Now, if the Bible tells us that we have to do everything we do, whether word or deed, "in the Name of the Lord Jesus," does that mean that we have received power of attorney to act for Jesus? Does it mean that I can act on the behalf of Jesus Christ Himself? Does it mean that I should do things *as if* I am Jesus, not that I am indeed Jesus, but that I am representing Him?

I went to see my pastor about it. I asked him these questions. He gave me a run down on some things, but affirmed to me - the bottom line was, *yes* that is what it means.

This had a great impact on me.

I began to think of how I would act if I was Jesus. Sometimes I would go sit in solitude some place outside, and think of what it would be like if I indeed *was* Jesus. I would sit there and pray until a consciousness came upon me of what it would be like if I was Jesus. Other times, that consciousness would not come on me, so I just went my way till next time. But oftentimes, I began to feel what it must be like to have been Jesus.

Obviously, I am not Jesus. Jesus is the *Only Begotten Son of God.* Jesus is *Jehovah God* Himself in the flesh. Jesus is God Almighty, who became a man.

But there is a wonderful, mystical oneness with Jesus for those who believe in Jesus.

Many years later, I was fasting in preparation for our first really big crusade in India. It was in 2001. I had a very curious experience, and I still can't connect all the dots. Our oldest son Anthony was at the age that he could climb out of his crib, and everyone knows – the day is about to get busy.

During that fast, after many days of drinking water only, I heard steps coming down the hallway. I was convinced it was Anthony. But suddenly, whoever it was, took me by the feet, and pulled my feet up into the ceiling. I realize this was a spirit, and I began to call out the Name of Jesus. At first, I could not say His

Name, but the more I tried, the stronger I got, and eventually could say it, "JESUS!"

Then the spirit let go of me, and departed in a flash.

At that moment, Heidi woke me saying, "Are you okay?" I could not believe I had just had a dream. I really thought that all of this happened in real life. I had never had a dream that felt so real, like in real life, and I have not had one like that since.

That day, I prayed about the dream. Suddenly I heard the voice of the Lord. "What is your desire number one for 2001? I began to think of the crusade, for the souls, for miracles and healing. But then the Lord interrupted my thinking. He said, "Your desire number one for 2001 is to become like the Son."

I think the reason the Lord gave this mandate to me in words that rhyme, is for me to remember it better.

It was with this mandate that I went to India for our first really big crusade. When I stepped on the platform, I felt like Jesus Himself was stepping onto the platform. When I preached, or when I laid hands onto the sick, it was to me as if Jesus was doing those things through me.

I later wrote a book on this concept, titled, "Christ in You – Experience the Power of Oneness with God." Reinhard Bonnke wrote the forward to it.

Becoming like Jesus is not a one-time experience. It is a continuous journey, and I have so far to still go.

Paul wrote about it when he said, "Christ in you, the hope of glory" (Colossians 1:17.)

Jehovah Incarnate

When I wrote the book, *Christ in You,* I first began to write about Jesus – for if we are to be like Jesus, what was He like? This became two books, the latter being *Jehovah Incarnate – Jesus Christ – God in the Flesh*. I experienced a wonderful new revelation of Jesus Christ. It took my 12 years to complete, not that I was writing every day, but I was studying the life and identity of Jesus in a deeper way than ever before.

Of course, I had always preached Jesus, but I began to really realize how amazing and great He was and is! As I studied Jesus, it began to amaze and fascinate me that Jesus is the almighty God and creator. Sometimes we do not speak of Jesus as He really is.

The Bible says "In the beginning was the Word" (John 1:1,) and that "all things were made by Him..." (John 1:3.) The Bible says, "In the beginning God created the heaven and the earth" (Genesis 1:1.) This means that Jesus is the almighty, eternal God and creator who created the heaven and the earth, and made all things. John 1:14 says, "And the Word became flesh and dwelt among us, and we beheld His glory, the glory as of the only begotten of the Father, full of grace and truth." Jesus is the Word. Jesus is the almighty, eternal God. Jesus is the God whom created all things. And He became flesh and dwelt among us!

This is how amazing and great our Lord Jesus is. The Bible calls Him, "Our great God and Savior – Jesus Christ" (Titus 2:13,) and the King James Version says about Jesus, "God was manifest in the flesh" (1 Timothy 3:16.)

He was none other that the Great and Almighty Creator God – whom the Old Testament names as *Jehovah*. This Almighty Jehovah became flesh, and called His Name JESUS, which means *Jehovah Savior*. Jesus is none other that Jehovah in the flesh, or as I put it, *Jehovah Incarnate*.

John 12:41 says that Isaiah saw Jesus' glory. Isaiah saw the glory of Jesus Christ! But when did He see Jesus' glory? We read about it in Isaiah 6 where it says, "In the year that King Uzziah died, I saw the Lord sitting on a throne, high and lifted up, and the train of His *robe* filled the temple. Above it stood seraphim;

each one had six wings: with two he covered his face, with two he covered his feet, and with two he flew. And one cried to another and said: "Holy, holy, holy *is* the Lord of hosts; The whole earth *is* full of His glory!" And the posts of the door were shaken by the voice of him who cried out, and the house was filled with smoke. So I said: "Woe *is* me, for I am undone! Because I *am* a man of unclean lips, And I dwell in the midst of a people of unclean lips; For my eyes have seen the King, The Lord of hosts" (Isaiah 6:1-5, NKJV.)

Isaiah said that his eyes had seen, "the King, the Lord," i.e. the King Jehovah (in Hebrew, Yahweh." John wrote that when this happened, Isaiah had seen JESUS' glory. John said that Jesus was this Great King Jehovah.

In Revelation we read about Jesus, "Now I saw heaven opened, and behold, a white horse. And He who sat on him *was* called Faithful and True, and in righteousness He judges and makes war. His eyes *were* like a flame of fire, and on His head *were* many crowns. He had a name written that no one knew except Himself. He *was* clothed with a robe dipped in blood, and His name is called The Word of God. And the armies in heaven, clothed in fine linen, white and clean, followed Him on white horses. Now out of His mouth goes a sharp sword, that with it He should strike the nations. And He Himself will rule them with a rod of iron. He Himself treads the winepress of the fierceness and wrath of Almighty God. And He has on *His* robe and on His thigh a name written: KING OF KINGS AND LORD OF LORDS" (Revelation 19:11-16, NKJV.)

And it describes Him is brilliant majesty, ""Then I turned to see the voice that spoke with me. And having turned I saw seven golden lampstands, and in the midst of the seven lampstands *One* like the Son of Man, clothed with a garment down to the feet and girded about the chest with a golden band. His head and hair *were* white like wool, as white as snow, and His eyes like a flame of fire; His feet *were* like fine brass, as if refined in a furnace, and His voice as the sound of many waters; He had in His right hand seven stars, out of His mouth went a sharp two-edged sword, and His countenance *was* like the sun shining in its strength (Revelation 12:12-17, NKJV.)

What a glorious, majestic God – Jesus Christ, God in the Flesh, Jehovah Incarnate.

Revelation 22:6 says that "the Lord God of the holy prophets sent His angel." Who was "the Lord God of the holy prophets?" He was Jehovah God of the Old Testament. It was this Jehovah God who sent His angel. But watch! Verse 16 identifies Jehovah God with Jesus Christ, because it says that the Lord God of the holy prophets who sent His angel is Jesus who sent His angel. It says, "I, Jesus, have sent My angel" (Revelation 22:16.)

I have intentionally written about Jesus as Jehovah Incarnate in this chapter of my testimony, because it is huge – it is an integral, inseparable part of my life and testimony. I wrote a 300-page book titled *Jehovah Incarnate,* about my Lord Jesus. In it, I cover Him from all the way back in eternity before creation, when it was *just Him out there*, to when He created everything, interacted with man throughout history, and eventually became flesh – Jehovah Incarnate. I then continue about Him – His sinless life, His teaching, and His miracles. And about His powerful, atoning death on the cross, and His glorious resurrection, ascension to heaven, and glorification, and His ultimate future coming.

It is for Him, and in Him, that I live, and move and have my being (Acts 17:26.)

My life and testimony are all about Jesus – God in the flesh, and His engagement with humanity.

I want to serve Him with a passion. There is no price too big to pay. We cannot be lukewarm or cold. The only service to God that counts is total surrender, zero compromise, and on-fire passion.

The future

I feel like I am in the prime of my life. None of us know the future, how long any of us will still be living, whether we be young or old.

On the inside I am bursting with passion to continue to share Jesus with our generation.

I will continue to do what God had called me to at an early age – to spread the Gospel of our Lord Jesus Christ, and do so with God confirming the Word with signs following.

Among others, I will continue to emphasize salvation through the atoning death and resurrection of Jesus Christ, physical healing and miracles in His Name, and the baptism in the Holy Spirit, with the speaking in tongues. I will also preach and teach about the power of faith in God.

I truly want people to experience God in the Person of Jesus Christ, in the power of the Holy Ghost.

This is my way of *Knowing God, and Making Him Known.*

Other

- Suggested prayer of salvation
- What to do now?
- About the Author
- Photo Album
- Contact information
- Scripture References

Suggested prayer of salvation

You may pray this following prayer as a guideline:

"Dear God. I am a sinner. I cannot save myself. I need a Savior, and your name is Jesus. Thank you, God, that you came to earth to reach me and to save me. Forgive me of all my sin and wash me clean with the precious blood of Jesus,

I believe with my heart and confess with my mouth that Jesus died and rose again. I further declare that Jesus is my Lord from this day forward forever. You are my only God.

I open my life to you. Lord Jesus, come live in my heart. Please give me the power of your Spirit that I may live righteously. Thank you for giving me eternal life, and that when I die I will meet Jesus and live in heaven with you forever.

In Jesus' name I pray, Amen…"

What to do now?

Congratulations on receiving Jesus as your Lord and Savior him now lives in your heart and you have received eternal life.

Now it is important that you grow in your faith and in your journey with God:

- Tell several people that you have received Jesus Christ – not only will this one simple act give you a spiritual growth spurt, but it will give them an opportunity to receive Jesus too;
- Be baptized by immersion, according to Matthew 28:19 and Acts 2:38 – in the name of the Father, Son and Holy Spirit and in the name of Jesus Christ;
- Find a powerful, enthusiastic church that preaches the Bible without compromise, and attend it regularly;
- Seek earnestly to be baptized in the Holy Spirit and power – which is a glorious experience accompanied by the speaking in tongues as in Acts 1:5-8 and 2:1-4;
- Obtain a Bible (digital or paper,) and read it daily – if you read 3 chapters a day you will complete it in a year;
- Pray daily – set aside a special time of your day for you and God, and also pray throughout the day (talk to God as if he's your friend;)
- Refrain from old sinful habits like bad language and substance abuse – avoid the places and people who discourage your faith;
- Make Christian friends that build you up and encourage you – they need you as much as you need them!

About the author

Joel Hitchcock is a pastor and evangelist. *Knowing God and Making Him Known* is his driving passion.

Joel is married to Heidi and they have four children - Anthony, Rebekah, Timothy, and Trey.

For over 30 years, Joel has preached the Good News of salvation, healing, and the Holy Spirit all around the world - in more than 45 countries. Multitudes have attended his mass evangelism miracle campaigns.

Joel has authored several books.

Joel also maintains his blog and YouTube channel as an extension of his ministry

- www.joelhitchcock.blogspot.com
- www.youtube.com/joelhitchcock

Having completed is doctoral thesis on *The Deity and Humanity of Jesus Christ,* Joel's great passion is centered around the Person of Jesus Christ, and our union with him.

Photo Album

First missions outreach: Preaching on the back porch of my parents' house

Preaching on the street corners of Pretoria

Carried a cross into a communist event and preached

The Yamaha XT 500 I used to travel from Johannesburg to Dar es Salaam and back to preach the Gospel Preaching the Gospel

Joel ministering in a village in Africa

One of Joel & Heidi's day-time meetings at the bus stop / market in Malawi – the crowd size increased at night. In time, our meetings would be quite larger all around the world.

The Great 20,400 Ft Gospel Tent, Delaware USA

Joel with Evangelist Nicky van der Westhuizen Sr.

Being dedicated to the Lord by Brother Nicky

Joel with Evangelist Reinhard Bonnke

Joel with Rodney Howard-Browne

Left: With my uncle - Evangelist John Hitchcock. Right: My cousin and I as kids in front of his church in Masvingo, Zimbabwe.

Joel & Heidi Hitchcock – June 3, 1995

L-R: Ronald & Linda Souder, Joel, Elaine & Tony Hitchcock

Joel & Heidi

Newlyweds & early years

On the Choptank River with our travel trailer home

Heidi's parents: Ron & Linda Souder

Joel's parents: Tony & Elaine Hitchcock

Joel Hitchcock, USA

Heidi Hitchcock, USA

Joel preaching in an Indian Village

Heidi preaching in an Indian Village

Indian Village

Warangal, India

Suryapet, India

Huzurnagar, India

Warangal, India

Miryalguda, India

Kothagudem, India

Halia, India

Joel at Reinhard Bonnke's Gospel campaign in Nigeria

Sialkot, Pakistan

Tucupita, Venezuela

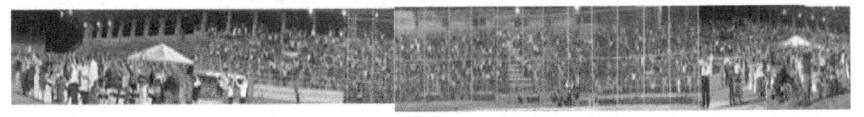

Other, Venezuela (Valencia?)

Suryapet, India

Douala, Cameroon

Joel Hitchcock, Florida – USA

Joel Hitchcock – Suryapet, India

Joel Hitchcock – Suryapet, India

Joel Hitchcock – Gulu, Uganda

Joel Hitchcock, Delaware – USA

Joel, Heidi, Anthony, Rebekah, Timothy, and Trey Hitchcock

Joel & Heidi Hitchcock

Contact information

Joel Hitchcock Ministries,
PO Box 936, Georgetown DE 19947
United States of America

302-858-0887

www.joelhitchcock.com
www.joelhitchcock.blogspot.com
www.youtube.com/joelhitchcock

Made in the USA
Middletown, DE
30 August 2023